SOBER SLOGANS

Recovery Mottos We Love

JEFF VICKERS

Sober Slogans

Recovery Mottos We All Love

First published by Sober Slogans 2021

Cover designed by Pro_ebookcovers.

Manufactured in the United States of America.

ISBN 978-1-7371940-0-2
ISBN 978-1-7371940-1-9 (ebook)

To my best friend, lover, business partner and Queen-Sassy. I am grateful that you allowed me to share in the experience of becoming you. All hail the Queen.

To my Queen mother, V-Dub, Precious, Vera Anne. Mama I made it...

To my children, who suffered the loss of me not being there because I didn't know who I was. I pray my future love can make up for the lost time...

CONTENTS

Introduction

"Success is the sum of small efforts,
repeated day in and day out."

—Robert Collier

Hello, my name is Jeff Vickers. I am a: Recovering Addict, Sober Enthusiast, Writer, Scriptwriter in the making, Hip Hop Junkie, Pescatarian, and "Star Wars" Lover.

Thank you for buying "Sober Slogans: Recovery Mottos We Love." I honestly love sobriety. Of course, there was a time this was not the case. Since the age of 15 I've struggled with addiction in one form or another; mainly crack.

My drug addiction has been about loss. I have lost years of growth being in prison, on three separate occasions. I have lost opportunities to bond with family. I've also lost friends through their drug addiction, so I know the struggle.

Initially I set out to write a memoir about my trials with drugs and what I've learned in the process. I finally "got" what sobriety is about and believed I could share a little of what I knew. But writing a dry memoir just didn't sit well with me. I didn't feel like I would be adding any value to another addict's life like that. Maybe I was wrong. I couched the idea and knew I would find my voice in due time. Then it hit me.

While in a treatment facility, attending the weekly N.A. meeting, I had a beautiful experience. As a result, an idea took shape.

For most of the members that night, it was their home group. Many of the people had been attending for years. They were friends and knew of each other's struggles and successes.

The excitement for me was knowing that it was a celebration meeting. Some had 5 years, a few had close to 10 years. I think the "oldest" celebrant had more than 25 years in recovery!

It was festive, and the spiritual energy spoke to me. There were multiple speakers celebrating their friends' accomplishments and embarrassments. That's what friends do.

That was the first meeting I attended where I truly saw the compassion and love of one addict helping another. Maybe my insight had something to do with the fact that I was finally serious about my recovery. It was beautiful and to this day has been my favorite meeting.

Genuine love. That's what I thought to myself, while I ate a piece of cake. I was seeing and feeling the genuine love these addicts had for one another.

While I listened to the celebrants and their peers, something struck me as odd. I noticed these addicts really enjoyed their "slogans." It seemed like everyone had a favorite saying. I just call them "sober slogans."

I've been to meetings where people threw sober slogans into their dialogue, but this was different. It seemed like no matter who was speaking, if someone threw out a slogan, the rest of the group chimed in. It seemed instinctual.

In the past I attended meetings that were, what I labeled as, overzealous. You know those meetings where the speaker shares, then before passing the mic, says something like, "Keep coming back," and the rest of the group repeats it?

That particular night I didn't think they were being overzealous. And I haven't thought that since. That night I realized that I've also used those slogans.

After the meeting I couldn't stop thinking about the power of these slogans. The cool thing is how prominent some of these sayings are. People who aren't even in recovery are familiar with sober slogans.

I'm the kid from the Bronx who grew up on Hip Hop and the love of language. I can walk on any street in Queens and know exactly what it means when I hear someone say, "Yo, what up, son?" It's the same if I stood in front of a bodega in the Bronx and a youngster said, "Yo, what up, B?"

We all understand lingo. The more cultural experience you have, the more you can relate to different cultures, or even the same culture, when spoken to in their lingo. There's power in lingo.

The power of sober slogans lies in the spiritual meaning of the words.

Let's say someone just relapsed, and they're attending their first meeting. Hearing something like: "Keep coming back," makes a difference. It signals empathy, and camaraderie.

So, it became clear that I had found my voice. I had to write a series on 'sober slogans.' My goal is to provide a recovery companion tool.

I believe, "Sober Slogans: Recovery Mottos We Love," serves three groups of people:

The Newcomer. Anyone just coming in the rooms can easily feel out of place. Starting the journey of sobriety is frightening. It is overwhelming. Going to meetings, The Big Book, The 12-Steps, The 12 Traditions—it's all part of a new lifestyle. "Just for today," "One day at a time," "Keep coming back," are all new lingos. Learning the terms of recovery is like learning a new language. When you know the language of the land, you feel less lost and relevant. Having a resource to pull from empowers the newcomer.

Friends and Family. This series can work two ways for friends and family. It can serve as a gift for someone in recovery; showing them the support they so desperately need. It can also be used as a relational tool for those supporting a recovering addict. These slogans are empowering to the recovering addict. They are positive affirmations, holding power for the addict who lives by them. Knowing what it means when you hear a struggling addict whisper, "Just for today," is invaluable.

The Clinician. Having source material for the client is a must. A few copies in a practitioner's library will service many. Each book in this series can serve as material for group discussions, personal exercises, and journaling. Clients equipped with recovery terminology have a better chance at survival. If *"language is the roadmap of a culture,"* then 'sober slogans' may very well be the dialect of recovery.

Thank you again for buying my book. This is the first of a series. I suggest you pick up a few copies.

Keep Coming Back

"Fall seven times and stand up eight."

—Japanese Proverb

Why we Fail

Want to know one of the greatest ironies in life? Failure is a predictor of success. I know it might seem unlikely, but it's actually true. And science backs me up on this. Instead of having a technical discourse on natural selection and evolution, I'll keep it simple. Simply put, we must fail—to succeed. Our brain is a problem-solver. On an individual level, that means each of us has the capacity to learn from our mistakes. But, to do so, we must fail (make a mistake), first.

Just analyze the stages of human motion. There are a lot of bumps and bruises along the way. As babies, we are immobile, then we crawl, until we can stand, walk, then eventually run. The fundamental stages of human mobility have intrinsic learning points or mistakes. This is for the sole purpose of learning how to move independently. We must fail.

Feeling Pain until we Learn

Most people don't like to fail, and that's understandable. We look at ourselves as losers and not worthy when we fail, especially addicts. But the thing is, all of us must and will fail. By now, as adults, we should understand this. The knowledge of this doesn't necessarily make us "feel" better, now does it? I know I've failed a lot, on so many levels in my life, and I'll fail again.

Thank you Grandma

My grandmother wasn't to be played with. She believed in "feeling the pain, until you learn." Full disclosure, I was a knucklehead. I didn't like to listen. I didn't like "authority figures," and I thought I was smarter than most. It took me years to understand some of her sayings. Well, I finally understand what she meant about "feeling the pain." That was her way of saying I had to learn from my mistakes. Thank you for the lessons, grandma. I finally got it.

Thank you Russell Brand

Initially I was going to list celebrities who struggled with drug addiction and alcoholism. Instead of that mundane approach, I'd rather briefly talk about just one "celebrity" and hopefully inspire you to check his book out.

I'm talking about Russell Brand, the comedian. I don't really like his voice, but I do enjoy his humor. He's not as great as Dave Chappelle or George

Carlin. But I enjoy comedians who can edutain me with intelligent social commentary. I knew about his struggles but didn't follow him. Now I do, thanks to his book, *"Recovery: Freedom from Our Addictions."*

I found the book during a ten-day stay at Dekalb Crisis Center. By the time I got there I was full of angst and despair. I aborted from the program 'Sober Living of America' in Dunwoody, GA. Without sugar-coating the situation, the so-called recovering addicts and staff were using. I refused to "pay" to live in a drug-infested environment. So, I took the advice of a friend and checked into Dekalb Crisis Center.

Aside from the N.A. and A.A. "big" books, I hadn't read anything on recovery. But I read Russell Brand's book, and still am. His insight is refreshing, and I appreciate him for giving back. I highly recommend this book to all addicts, of all forms.

Dekalb Crisis Center
While curled up under two thin, itchy blankets—courtesy of Dekalb County—I ignored my roommate's weepy monologue. His girlfriend was cheating while he was "drying out." I consoled him here and there but really... I figured it was best for me to mind my business. I can be a little too blunt sometimes, so....

I flipped through the pages like it was pulp fiction! Russell's no-nonsense approach to recovery totally debunked my fears and preconceptions. (When the student is ready, the teacher will appear.) I believe he had me in mind when he wrote his book. I was a tepid, struggling, newcomer in recovery, looking for wisdom.

By stripping away his ego, he imparted a comically pragmatic understanding of the spiritual principles of recovery. I want to share the number one lesson I've learned so far.

Russell Brand has been sober for 17 years. Gone are the days of Mr. Brand desensitizing himself with heroin, crack, alcohol, sex, and chocolate biscuits. The concept that initiated his sober journey and what has kept him sober, is the belief that he has the capacity to live addiction free. I'm not talking about a "little engine that could" surface belief. I'm talking about a deep understanding that he first had to "believe" he could live at least *one* day clean. This reminds me of one of my favorite movies. But first...

C-Town

I grew up with my maternal grandmother in the Bronx. Grandma would periodically give me an allowance. To be honest, my behavior wasn't consistent enough to keep free money coming in. By the time I was old enough to go to the movies by myself, I had the determination of a hustler.

My best friend, Damon Williams, was also a hustler. This is the guy who introduced me to packing bags for tips. Saturdays was movie day. On Saturday mornings and afternoons, we'd pack bags at C-Town. Damon was so good he was able to double-pack, at the same time. His skills were phenomenal. Packing bags might not seem like a refined skill set, but this guy was the best! He was the fastest, and his bags were packed with such density, it was incredible.

His "density" approach was based on the game "Tetris." We both loved that game, so when he explained his methodology, it made perfect sense. I can still remember him saying, "Don't leave any spaces." We'd lined the bottom of the brown paper bags with appropriately sized cans about half-way up, then top the other half of the bags with fruits, vegetables, or whatever. And of course, we would double up with plastic bags for stability. We did alright for ourselves. That's how we made our movie money. And we both loved the same movies.

The Empire Strikes Back

I've always had a thing for stories. Big elaborate stories. Adventures. Sagas. We've been telling stories to explain our views of the world for years. From the oral histories of Ethiopia to the hieroglyphics of Egypt to the scrolls of the Romans— humanity has always loved a good story.

I do love books, but I LOVE movies. To see an author's written imagery in your mind is a beautiful thing. But to "see" how a director and cinematographer visually display words from a script? That's just amazing to me.

I'm almost 50, so I grew up on *"The Goonies," "E.T.," "Time Bandits,"* and of course, my favorite, *"Star Wars."*

I love what they're doing these days, but my favorite installment is still *"The Empire Strikes Back."* My favorite scene in the movie is when Yoda is training Luke in the swamp. This is a famous scene and I know much has been written about it. However, I believe this is a perfect example for my point.

The X-Wing Fighter

If I could retitle this scene, it would be: "When You Believe in Yourself, You Can Do Anything." So...

Yoda and Luke are in a swamp and Luke's aircraft, the "X-Wing Fighter," has sunk into the swamp. Yoda's ongoing job is to give Luke lessons on the power of the "Force." Each Jedi-in-training receives lessons from a mentor Jedi. Up until this point, Luke has learned how to move small objects with the power of his mind. Yoda now wants to show Luke just how powerful the Force is.

Luke explains that moving stones with his mind is one thing but lifting an aircraft out of a swamp is something entirely different. With a heavy heart and the single tap of his staff, Yoda admonishes Luke for his lack of belief. The ancient, green Jedi tells his stubborn mentee the "difference" lies only in his mind, and that he must "unlearn what he has learned."

Being the pessimistic prince that he is, Luke replies that he'll "try." (By this point Yoda has already given Luke enough spiritual food to last a lifetime, but his job isn't done until Luke genuinely believes in the Force.)

With half-hearted belief Luke proceeds to lift the aircraft. Yoda's eyes do the speaking for him. They cheer Luke on, with pride and wonder, but Luke's belief in himself evaporates. Seeing that his pupil has yet to embrace the power within, Yoda is dismayed. Luke pouts in self-defeat and walks away.

A lesson isn't taught until the student "sees" the answer. Since Yoda is aware of this precept, he not only lifts the aircraft, but pulls it toward them and gently lets it down on the soil. Luke is astonished and simply comments, "I don't believe it," to which Yoda sadly replied, "That is why you fail."

The Greatest Fight

I believe our greatest fight is the one that lies within. I've battled addiction since I was 15 years old. That's over 30 years, and if you've struggled like I have, then you know what fight I'm talking about.

This fight, this war—is the greatest saga that could ever be told. Like I said, I love stories, but MY STORY is the one that I've come to treasure the most. And you should treasure your own story the most, as well.

There are two sides to this fight. One side, (The Force), is connected to the energy within that enables us to be great. The other side, (The Dark Side), is connected to the energy within that urges us to self-destruct. This is the plight and miracle of humanity.

When you're fighting a war, I think the saddest thing is not knowing who the enemy is.

During my active addiction I played both sides. Rather—until sobriety—I played on the wrong side, believing certain actions won a battle here, and a battle there. All along I fought for the wrong side.

There were times I'd go months without smoking crack. I didn't understand the enemy back then, so I thought smoking weed and drinking was cool for me. I believed that I was winning. I believed I was on the right side of the fight. I gained a few pounds. I wasn't selling all my stuff. Nobody was after me. I was winning, right? Not even close.

There were even days I'd flip sides during the *same* day. One minute I'd exclaim victory. In that moment of clarity, I'd throw away all my paraphernalia. Soon after though, I'd be right back out there chasing the next hit. The struggle was real. I was just like Luke in that swamp.

The Greatest Question

Why does Russell Brand have almost two decades clean? Why couldn't Luke Skywalker lift his aircraft out of the swamp? It's called belief, self-belief, to be specific. One had it. One didn't.

Now, of course, Russell Brand had to slum through his own 'swamps' until he got it right. In his book he explains that he scrutinized recovery. He also scrutinized the likelihood of true sobriety in such a messed-up world. But most importantly, he scrutinized himself.

Luke Skywalker also scrutinized everything around him. Question after question, goes the curious mind. Yoda had to tell Luke to stop questioning the outside and allow his mind to travel inward. So, Luke began to question himself. Why did he have so little belief in "The Force?"

Anyone who's been on this road to recovery knows just how scary self-evaluation is. I've traveled the road of self-discovery since I was a teen. I've been an orthodox Muslim, a born-again Christian, and a Five Percenter. I've prayed up to five times a day, fasted for holidays, and meditated. I've read literature from Sophocles, Socrates, Dumas, Shakespeare, Milton, Che, Marx, Rogers, Akbar, Welsing, and others.

While learning from these intellects, I have argued, debated, judged, compromised, and even protested. I was searching for the great meanings of life. Since life is a classroom, I've learned from fables, great philosophers and even men who would die in prison. Of all the questions asked, it became clear that the greatest question is "why?"

Why am I an addict? Why can't I stop destroying my life? Why don't I believe in myself?

The 13th Floor

Grady hospital is a famous hospital located in downtown Atlanta. People in Atlanta will proudly tell you they are "a Grady baby." No kidding.

After trying to commit suicide on the last night of my drug use, I was admitted to Grady's psychiatric unit, which is on the 13th floor. Historically, the number 13 is said to be an "unlucky" numeral. Well, I began my journey of recovery on the 13th floor.

During my few days there I began to question my sanity. Coming off that binge was a harrowing experience. There were moments when I felt like I was losing my mind. Then there were moments when it felt like I was as smart as Elon Musk.

All I wanted to do was sleep. Being awake was torture. I couldn't stop asking myself "why?" I wanted to run from that question, a question my subconscious was increasingly turning up in my head, like decibels on a stereo. "Why?" Why couldn't I stop this self-destructive, downward spiraling, internal self-combusting life? Why have I allowed crack to control me for three decades? Why did I hate myself so much? The reality of my plight literally made my body shake. I cried. I cried a lot.

Drama on the 13th Floor

Since I was on the "psych unit," you can imagine the opportunities for drama. Surprisingly, there weren't many incidents. But there was one that became a pivotal point for my growth.

There was an older white man who liked to control the TV. There was also a young black man who didn't like that, especially since there was only one white guy on the unit. The young black man expressed his discontent. Surprisingly, the younger man was respectful, at first. (Keep in mind, we were on the "psych" unit in Grady hospital.) The conversation rapidly deteriorated into racist slurs. After the older white man was escorted off the unit, we helped ourselves to the forgotten snacks.

After the remote found a new owner, I went through an interesting process. While in prison, I witnessed a lot of ignorance, especially over the TV. I was

10

relieved that the situation on the unit didn't turn violent. I think it would've, though. The ordeal was handled rather quickly, but it made me think. What the hell was I doing in another institution over drug use?

Did I really think so little of myself that I was willing to keep reliving past scenarios? Would I ever pull myself up from this reenactment of Riker's Island? Wasn't I tired of torturing myself? When would I stop viewing myself as a loser?

Then it hit me. It was the question that started my journey to recovery. *"Why don't you stop killing yourself and see how far you can go by living?"*

This question crept up from my belly and reached my eyes. I perched a leg onto a plastic chair and stared at downtown Atlanta. That night I made a promise to myself. I promised that I would spend the rest of my life sober, no matter what.

Lucky Me

I hadn't prayed in some time, but I did that night.

I had no idea I was getting released the next day, but I woke up early and watched the sun rise. I woke up with a promise still in my heart. Watching downtown Atlanta wake up is a beautiful sight. I observed the Sun swallow the shadows on the buildings below. It was like watching a time-lapse as the city woke up. The perfect song would have been Nina Simone's "Here comes the Sun." I felt alive! Watching the city come alive imbued me with

11

courage. Although I was on the 13th floor, I felt pretty lucky.

Walking out of Grady hospital was scary. I pushed through the revolving doors, wondering if the woman coming in could see my fear. My face expressed a pleasant smile, but my heart was pounding. I immediately bummed a cigarette and felt sick to my stomach after I smoked it. With sweaty hands I tapped the crumbled-up discharge papers on my thigh and walked to the bus station.

I was homeless once again. My ex-girlfriend had my clothes, but there was no way I was going back there. Her and her daughter were still using. They were the functional addicts. I was not.

Marta Bus with God

I hopped on the bus, thinking it was best to go back to MUST Ministries. I completed the program and thought I was eligible for a second round of help. Connecting my shattered phone to the MARTA bus's wi-fi, I screenshot directions. Then I cried.

I couldn't help the fear in my chest or the tears dropping onto my beat-up jeans. I flipped to a photo album for a little solace. I needed to see pictures of when I looked "like somebody." My inner "Vanity Smurf" thought this would do the trick. It didn't.

Although I looked good in the pictures, most of them were taken when I was high out of my mind. I still looked better in them than I did that day on the bus. I actually had "cheeks" in most of the pictures. Self-consciously running my right hand from my cheeks to my chin, I couldn't help thinking my face looked like an isosceles triangle.

Keep coming back. The thought hit me so suddenly, it made me sit up and wipe away the tears. I nervously peeked around to see if someone on the bus said this. Nope. *That definitely came from my mind,* I thought. I chose to believe it was a message from God.

The reality of me crying on the bus with a phone in my hand and hearing from God made me laugh. That's when I noticed a young woman shake her head at me while exiting the bus. I stuck my tongue out at her and went back to looking at my photos.

A Lovely Song

I had a long trek to get back to MUST Ministries. It felt like I was back in New York. I had to take two trains and two buses. *Keep Coming Back.* Like a song from the mythical 'Siren,' those words looped inside my head like a melody, pulling me forward. The train rolled into stations that were a trigger for me, especially Five Points. (Anyone from Atlanta knows about that area.) But the song kept me moving forward. *Keep Coming Back.*

Over the years I heard this saying in meetings. At times I piped in with everyone else, but on that day a new meaning developed. By the time I sat on the last bus, I was tired of the repetition. But a memory came to me and the dreaded song was at the center of the message.

Josh—The Sponsor

Back in the winter of 2019, Memorial Drive was one my "stomping grounds." My headquarters was a certain motel. Next to the drug infested motel was a small plaza. Inside the plaza, tucked in the left corner, was an A.A. home group.

After being heavily marketed to for a few months, I took the bait. I joined the sober living community and gave a half-hearted effort to stay clean. To be honest, I joined because I was tired of being awaken by police. I was illegally sleeping inside buildings. I needed a place to stay. Within a week I left the program and was right back in that plaza selling stolen merch to the Muslims.

It was impossible to hide from "the A.A. guys." The plaza was small, and I was popular. My recent ex-sponsor was a guy named Josh. He was a mild-mannered, down to earth guy. I avoided him for weeks. One night he jogged toward me waving his arms. I couldn't ignore the guy.

My pocket burned with the few dollars in it, waiting to go up in smoke. But I respected the guy and had to at least allow him the opportunity to hit me with his spiel.

He forked over a cigarette before I could ask. Respecting my embarrassment, he avoided eye contact and feigned interest in the couple arguing across the street. Since he already knew what I was doing, he asked a simple question, "How are you feeling?" I told him the truth, while I caressed the pipe in my left pocket. I felt like shit.

It just started but the chat was lasting way too long. Josh didn't keep me long. He knew what I was going through. He used to smoke crack. I would have never guessed, but that's just how deceitful this addiction is. I cut Josh off as respectfully as I could. He didn't mind, though. He flicked a cigarette, then felt guilty about not offering it to me.

For the first time he looked at me directly, violating our unspoken agreement. Subconsciously he nodded his head as he said, "You know you can come back, right?" After watching so many episodes of *"Lie to Me,"* I trusted his earnestness, since his words and body language coincided.

I didn't even respond. My eyes probably did, though. Before leaving the scene, I swooped down and grabbed the cigarette he just tossed. From over my shoulder, Josh piped up, "Yo, Jeff, **keep coming back**!" I had no plans on taking up his offer.

This memory faded just before my stop. I smiled at the thought.

The Struggle is Real

If you're an addict, you know the struggle is real. The struggle of avoiding mirrors. The struggle that comes from knowing you are better than your addiction, but still haven't found the power within to quit. That is THE struggle.

I've known the push and pull of the will since I was 15 years old. I can't tell you how many times I've promised myself that "this" would be the last one. Or that "today" would be the last day.

Riding on the bus back to Must Ministries I knew I'd never get high again. I had a promise in my head and a song in my heart. I knew it was a long road ahead. I knew there would be plenty of opportunities to get high. But I also knew there would be plenty of opportunities not to get high. I would choose sobriety over anything else. No matter what.

Relapse Happens

I've heard it said that relapse is an option on the road to recovery, but it's not mandatory. After a five-year relapse binge, I was finally ready to get it together. Fresh out of the psych-unit, on my way to a safe-haven, the memory of Josh struck home. But why did my subconscious pull this memory forward?

Empathizing with my shame, Josh shouted, **"Yo, Jeff, keep coming back!"** But what was he really saying?

I believe this memory occurred because I needed reminding. The subconscious is tricky like that. Once again, I was feeling shame. I felt shame that day on the bus. And I felt it that night talking to Josh.

Shame has led me to relapse. Feeling shame, I believed there was no use in trying. My addiction used shame to lie to me. But you know what? There is no shame in the rooms of recovery. This is what Josh was telling me when I shuffled away.

Josh was informing me that I could come back. He was telling me that there is no judgement in recovery. With this simple statement Josh was telling me that he, and the addicts in the parking lot that night, had been where I was. And it was ok for me to come to the next meeting. It was ok for me to come back, because if I did, I would eventually "get it." If I kept coming back, the spiritual principles of recovery would eventually take hold.

Have you heard about the guy with unkept hair that kept going to the barbershop? He eventually got a haircut, right? Well, the same principle applies for the addict who has relapsed. Just *"keep coming back,"* no matter how many times it takes to get sober. Just *"keep coming back,"* and eventually the message will take root.

Self-Belief

Most people in recovery have relapsed. If you've been addicted for some time, it may honestly take a few relapses. You don't have to, but it does happen. At some point, if you want to embrace that better version of yourself, you've got to move forward. This coming-of-age moment can only happen if you believe. **YOU MUST BELIEVE THAT YOU CAN!**

I was only able to make a promise to God and myself on the 13th floor because I believed. I believed I could live a life of sobriety. For years people told me how much "potential" I had. For years people tried to make me see that I was more than an addict. I've even had drug dealers stop selling to me because they believed in me! No, really. Of course, I just went to the next drug dealer. I didn't believe in myself enough to stop using.

Let me tell you once that belief sets in—watch out! When you have self-belief, nothing can stop you. And I mean, NOTHING! You can look upon **ANY** mountain and say, *"Move from me,"* and that mountain will have no choice.

So, you Relapsed?

What if you did relapse? Now what? Well, you have options. And having options is always a good thing. You can sulk about it and let the shame guide you to another relapse. Or you can go to a meeting. Whether that meeting is in person or a zoom meeting, you have options.

You must *"keep coming back."* I've endured many relapses. But remembering what my ex-sponsor said to me really helped. It was at least a year later, but it stuck. **"Yo, Jeff, keep coming back!"** I kept coming back and it's the only reason I'm sober today.

Don't let the shame of a relapse keep you using. Any day alive is as good a day as any to get sober. Let today be your day!

It took me over 30 years, but I'm sober today. And I'm sober because I wanted to heal. True recovery is about getting pass all the pain. The pain that made me feel inconsequential. The pain that kept me reliving childhood memories. But recovery? Now, that's about me becoming a better me. I couldn't do that while drinking and drugging. I had to keep coming back. In a sense, every day I'm sober, I *"keep coming back."*

I surround myself with people, places, and things that are healthy for me. I surround myself with reminders of where I want to be, who I want to be. Some days are easy. Some days are hard. But I *keep coming back* daily, to spiritual principles that elevate me. If I can do it, I know you can. It's a daily grind, just like anything else that's worth it. And I believe you are worth it. Now you need to believe you are worth it!

You can come back to the road of recovery and live a sober life. It is possible. It's just a meeting away. Meetings, no matter what form they are, is where the spiritual energy is. Meetings are to the newcomer, what water is to the seed. Without water a seed cannot grow. Without being surrounded by recovering addicts who understand the struggle, a newly relapsed addict will relapse again.

Choosing Sobriety

Please keep in mind, no matter how much clean time an addict has, relapse is always a decision away. Don't be fooled, even the person with 20 years clean *can* relapse. They're no different than you, in that regard. The thing is, the person with 20 years sober, chose to stay sober—for 20 consecutive years.

I'm personally scared of relapsing because I don't have an "off" button. My addiction is a beast. My addiction takes everything from me and everything out of me. For over 30 years I've tried to put the beast back in the cage. I tried my own "program," but nothing worked. Now I live by the spiritual principles I found in recovery. They work. I allow them to work. Because I know that *one is too many and a thousand is never enough....*

One Is Too Many and A Thousand Is Never Enough

"All limits are self- imposed."

—Icarus

We need Reminders

As a recovering addict, it's important for me to never forget where I came from. I'm not talking about the projects. I'm not talking about the prisons I've been in. I'm talking about my addiction and where it led me. So, I need daily reminders. What we forget, we repeat, right?

Based on my history, I know that if I choose to EVER smoke crack again, it will be the death of me. I know this because I can't stop when I start. No matter how many times I've lied to myself, history repeated itself. Once I get high, I can't stop. It took me years to realize that I'm "allergic" to all forms of mind-altering chemicals.

Stop Smoking Weed?

A few years ago I had a discussion with a friend of mine about why I shouldn't smoke weed. This woman has known me since childhood. Despite her intimate knowledge about my family's addictive dynamics and my personal struggles, I tried to debate with her. Of course, my reasoning was flawed. But what addict makes sense when they're trying to rationalize getting high?

You can imagine how I felt hearing her explain to me that weed is a "gateway" drug. We're roughly the same age and from the same projects. So, I found it interesting to hear her use a reference from our childhood.

At the time of the discussion, I only had a few weeks abstinence from smoking crack. (I was smoking weed all day long, though.) I sought a victory by using my best rhetoric, but she was relentless. I knew her argument was sound but didn't enjoy her using a federally sponsored reference. In addition, *she* smoked weed!

Truth be Told

Truth be told, it didn't matter how much weed she smoked, I was the addict. She had a successful life, I didn't. I know a lot of people who smoke weed all day, but they're successful. (Snoop Dogg, Wiz Khalifa, Bill Maher, and Michael Phelps, to name a few.) However, I was the addict who struggled for over 30 years, not her.

The truth is, I already knew this. I have always known this, no matter how much I wished it weren't true. I knew it was best for me to avoid any mind-altering chemical.

I also knew I had a "drug of choice," and would eventually seek that out. My history proved this. All addicts learn this through their behavior. For me, smoking weed was like drinking 2% milk, while crack was whole milk. At some point the craving for the real deal would kick in. It always did. I knew this. She knew this. And she knew that I knew.

The Cocaine Rat

Back in the late eighties there was an anti-drug campaign sponsored by the "Partnership for a Drug-Free America." These are the people who did the "This is Your Brain on Drugs" commercial with the fried egg. The same people did the "Cocaine Rat" commercials.

In one commercial we see a lab mouse eating pellets of cocaine until it overdoses. In another commercial—the one that burned in my brain—lab mice compulsively pressed a lever, which contained cocaine-laced water. The last frame of that commercial also ends with an overdose.

The point of the campaign was to show America cocaine kills. What stuck out for me was the "compulsion" of these mice. I couldn't understand why those stupid mice kept going back to the lever, knowing a fellow mouse just died! Funny thing is, it took over 30 years for me to realize that I was the cocaine mouse.

The Cycle of Compulsion

What is "compulsion?" It's when you have an irresistible urge to do something against your conscious wishes. This is like having a war go on in your mind. You don't *want* to do something, but you *have* to do it, although you really don't want to. Not only is the war in your mind, but your body follows the thought that's betraying you. That's war of a different kind. You know who the enemy is, but you can't stop them. If you've ever watched "My Strange Addiction," you know what I'm talking about.

Maybe the cocaine rats went through this. Maybe not. What I do know is, the emotional turmoil associated with addictive compulsion is no joke.

Anytime I've relapsed, I couldn't stop. I chose not to forget this simple truth. My addiction doesn't take breaks. My addiction doesn't slow down. I honestly have no control once I start. "A thousand is never enough" for me. I don't eat. I don't sleep. And I hardly even drink fluids. All I want to do is get high. Well, not anymore.

Binge Eating

I'm an addict. A recovering addict, but still an addict. Until I embraced sobriety, I desensitized my feelings with just about anything, including food. I've never been 'overweight,' but I've struggled with sweets for years.

In my last chapter I mentioned Russell Brand's struggle with chocolate biscuits. I happen to have a history with Snickers and Whatchamacallits.

I had my first experience with compulsive, binge eating when I was a teen. It was over a girl, of course. It was just me, a bag of Hershey's Kisses, and a Kung-fu flick.

I was hurt and needed solace. My happiness rested inside tin foil and was wrapped with a cute little label around it. I absentmindedly stuffed a few in my mouth back-to-back, then slowed down, just to repeat the stuffing. Maybe it was the 5th piece, maybe the 10th, but I recognized two things. I liked chocolate, but not *that* much. And I wanted to stop eating them but couldn't. (I've been binge eating chocolate since then, until recently.)

After hearing a female friend explain why she hated herself, I realized I had a problem. She was bulimic. Although she was a knockout, she had body issues. She was an aspiring actress and model who wanted to keep a "thin" figure, so she'd binge on food, then chuck it all up.

She regretted having a "tortuous, emotional cycle" associated with binge eating. Since she was light years ahead of me in the self-awareness department, I just listened. Then it occurred to me that I was also a binge eater. Not only that, but I also went through the same cycle with chocolate.

When I was feeling sad, I would pull out the chocolates. After gobbling too many, (and mentally calling myself "a gorge"), I'd feel regret, then desperation, only to seek happiness again. So, I'd pop another piece in my mouth. I was emotionally torturing myself. I didn't even want to keep eating, but I would. A moment of happiness was followed by negative emotions. Without meaning to, I was chasing happiness with food, until I found something else. (Little did I know, this was my first sign of addictive behavior.)

Mr. Tin Man

During my last relapse, I went through this cycle of compulsion with crack. I smoked until my body gave out. My body locked up on me due to severe dehydration.

My final relapse occurred on a scorching August day in Atlanta. It was so hot outside the prostitutes on Fulton Industrial Boulevard (F.I.B.) sat under pop-up tents. When a customer pulled up, the women collapsed their tent, then hopped in the car. I think the customers received a discount if they collapsed the tents. (Not that I was all in their business or anything.)

I ran back and forth from the Citgo to the BP, with no hat on. Since I wear a bald head, sweat collects on my eyebrows, then cascades onto my face. It looked like my whole face was raining. My socks and sneakers were soaked. I sloshed when I ran across the street. It was bone dry outside, but I was sloshing. One dealer said I loss so much weight that day, he only recognized me because I was sloshing.

When I stood up, I literally had to take both hands and force the back of my legs to move. If I wanted to bend down, I had to force my body down. I'm talking real-life Tin Man stuff here! My compulsion didn't fit hydration in the schedule.

The 'Resume' Button

I never want to feel that compulsion again. Now that I'm sober, I'm learning about this disease. Like, whenever I relapsed, I picked up right where I left off. It didn't matter if I didn't get high for years. It didn't matter what I accumulated during my "abstinence." I forfeited everything as soon as I relapsed. I might've finally gotten a job, and bought a wardrobe, but no matter how "good" I looked, I still felt ugly. And during those times, my addiction was just waiting for the right moment.

The "resume" button for addiction is like resuming a movie on Netflix. Most know, if you leave before a show is over, you can resume where you left off.

When I abstained from drugs, all I did was "pause" my addiction. Focusing on something else didn't cure me. That's not being in recovery. It only means I focused on another platform. My addiction knows the difference.

G-Money Relapsed

I have a friend we call "G-Money." Unfortunately, he relapsed after doing 3 months in treatment. His story shows just how cunning this disease of addiction is. This is a prime example of why, "One is too many and a thousand is never enough."

About two years ago, G-Money went into a treatment program. The program was for 6 months. But he convinced his girlfriend he was ready to leave after only 3 months. After some hesitation she agreed to let him come home.

G-Money is a nice-looking guy. When you put a guy like him in some nice-looking clothes, he's picture perfect. G-Money is the working type. He's not the type to sit around and do nothing. During his abstinence he hustled hard at his job. During this time, he was able to accumulate a few things. But what he didn't accumulate was enough sober time. So, he relapsed.

Fast forward to late 2020. G-Money went back into another treatment program. It just so happens this new program is a 6–12-month commitment. Once again, at the 3-month mark, G-Money believes he's ready to leave the program. Again, he convinces his girlfriend. What do you think happened?

Unfortunately, he repeated the behaviors of his last relapse—almost literally. He ran off with the car—again. He spent up all his money—again. He also went right back the same area. He perpetuated the same behavior. But why?

An Addict's Brain

How is this possible? Why did G-Money's addiction resume exactly where it left off? Because that's how addiction works. Essentially, all addictions are spiritually rooted. However, let's view this from a biological standpoint.

The brain's job is to record data and solve problems. In order to solve a problem, the brain has to have data to pull from. When we have a thought, and consistently react more or less the same way, we establish a pattern of behavior. That pattern between thought and behavior is a cycle. The brain records this cycle, and it becomes "wired."

To break a cycle of behavior, we must "rewire" our perspective. Then and only then can we expect a new pattern to develop.

This is why G-Money repeated his behaviors. He didn't replace his way of thinking with something new. In no way am I judging this guy. I went through that same cycle for years.

I've been to prison three times due to my drug addiction. My first two offenses were in Co-op City, in the Bronx, NY. Very few are aware that I was arrested by the same police on both occasions. Yep, after doing a short stint in prison, I came home and committed the same crime in the same area and was arrested by the same police. Not just the same police department, but *the same police officers.* I felt like an imbecile.

My brain was hardwired like a program, and addiction was the program. I perpetuated the same behaviors for years. However, that changed once I started to rewire my brain. And I only learned that through the process of recovery.

What is Recovery, Really?
Being in recovery means therapy. And many of us don't like therapy. I didn't grow up around people who went to therapy. If any of my peers went, I didn't know about it.

But I've learned that therapy helps. It helps even more once you understand what it's all about.

Without intending to demean the profession, here's my honest opinion.

Therapy, in the broad sense, is a practice that analyzes, diagnoses, and treats disorders. Treatment may or may not include prescribed medications.

The first thing a therapist does is collect data. This is the reason they ask all the questions, especially at the beginning of the relationship. They do this in order to build a profile. Most of us easily fall into predetermined profiles, based on quantified data from countless subjects. (We're not as different from each other, as we like to think.)

I've been to therapists, inside and outside of treatment facilities. Once the therapist has profiled us, they more or less know how to deal with our disorder.

Dialogue is conducted to collect data. Therapists listen with a learned ear. Their job is to find the meaning behind what we say. The more they're able to drill down our meanings, the easier it is to get to the root cause of our misperceptions.

After a few prolonged dialogue sessions, a therapist will prescribe homework. Homework is given to remedy the ailment through actionable steps. Believe it or not, the "ailment" is our self-perception. In short, how we think about ourselves. So, homework is given to assist us in rewiring our brain.

Addiction treatment facilities exist for the same reason. The number one priority of treatment is relapse prevention. The reason we're taught about triggers and the effects of drugs on the brain, is to rewire our brains. We must learn about the disease, then learn to think differently.

When I was in treatment, they enjoyed having us act out scenarios. I thought this was smart. We would read off scripts, then be asked to act out the appropriate reactions. Most of the skits centered on triggers and how to avoid relapse.

I was in treatment during the upcoming holidays. If I'm correct, Thanksgiving was approaching. We all know how festive the holidays are. And of course, when I say "festive," I mean partying.

So, the skits focused on how we'd react if we were asked to drink or use. Some of the characters knew we were in recovery. They purposely tempted us to relapse. Other characters didn't know about us being in recovery. They still attempted to party with us, albeit they had different motives. In either case, our job was to act out possible reactions.

The purpose of the skits was to rewire our reactions during the holidays. Like I said, the primary purpose of treatment is relapse prevention. If we don't take that first one, we won't have to worry about the next.

But what happens after treatment? How do we continue to rewire our brain? Do we need more training to prevent relapse? And if so, where do we get that training?

The 12-Steps

Treatment is like college. Their job is to overload us with information. Some of it will stick. Some of it won't. Our job is to absorb as much as we can. The hope is that we'll use what we learned, in the real world.

If I have a Masters degree in Business Management, I'll seek employment in the business sector. When I leave treatment, I should seek a life in sobriety.

In the business world there are "best practices." These are systems that have proven to be effective, efficient, and profitable. There's enough data out there to prove what works and what doesn't. This is also the case in the "sober" world. We call those best practices the "12-Steps."

I like to call the 12-Steps, "the blueprint." This is where we receive the rest of our training to stay sober. This is what's recommended to the recovering addict. If you're going to live a sober life, this is what to follow.

My mother has almost 20 years in sobriety. I don't know how many rounds she's made through the steps. But what I do know is, they've helped her stay sober. And they are helping me to stay sober. So, I plan on living by them for the rest of my life.

I don't intend to elaborate on any steps in particular. I only wish to implore you to live by these steps. They are enriching to any addict who lives by them. This is the blueprint that keeps us sober.

Each step challenges us to learn more about ourselves. Going through these steps enables us to become a better version. That's my goal: to be a better me. In order to do that I have to constantly self-evaluate. I have to be willing to see myself and the world around me, differently.

Investing in these steps makes it easier to avoid relapse. This is the blueprint lived out by millions of recovering addicts. Only by practicing the principles we learn from these steps can we avoid relapse. And once we stop living by them, even if it's 20 years later, we will inevitably pick up.

The goal is to live a life that reminds us that one is too many. The goal is to keep relapse from occurring, so we don't press the resume button in our brains. Because if we resume active addiction, I can only promise a thousand won't be enough. I can honestly promise you this.

Why we Crave

I'm 48 years old. My "active" days as an addict outweigh my "recovering" days. I've jacked my brain up with substances for years. Then I cut off the supply. So, some days my brain feels like something is "missing."

Random cravings are going to occur. We just have to get used to them. During moments of abstinence, cravings ruined my whole day. I've even relapsed by giving into cravings.

Just like we can't control random thoughts, we can't control random cravings. And there's no need to feel bad about this. It sucks. It really does. But knowing why they occur, empowers us to resist the urge.

Since the brain records sensory data, practically anything can trigger a craving. The smell of a hyacinth; the feel of a latex costume at DragonCon—anything is fair game. At any moment, our brain might connect a present moment with something from our past.

There could be underlying connections between seemingly unrelated events. But our brain will make that connection. That's what it does. Sometimes I try to figure out the connections. Other times I just let it go.

One craving in particular really annoyed me. With a pen and pad I wrote down everything I could recall, but to no avail. Until, by happenstance, I eventually found out...

I absolutely love pistachio ice cream. One day, while enjoying a delicious cone from Bruster's, I had a craving. One minute I'm thinking of my childhood, and the next I was smelling crack. That ruined everything, so I tossed the cone.

The thought of wasting a few bucks, riled me a little. But something else made me even more upset. I couldn't figure out why I had the craving. I've never had any episodes involving ice cream. As much as I tried, I couldn't figure it out. A few weeks passed, then it hit me.

During my active use, I'd frequent a certain Waffle House. Honestly, I'd get high in the bathroom. I just never got caught. Everyone there knew I was an addict, so they pitied me. Whenever I "looked normal," they'd throw me free meals.

On one of my normal-looking days, I conned a waitress out of some money. I promised to give her the money back. Of course, I had no intentions on paying her, since I was still using.

A few weeks after the 'ice cream' craving, I happened to be near that Waffle House. Since I was sober and feeling guilty, I had to pay the nice woman back. She's been working there for years, so I figured she'd be there. I was right. After my meal, I introduced myself to her. She was blown away. I knew I looked different being 30 pounds heavier.

The woman almost made me cry when I handed her fifty bucks. After breaking away from her prolonged embrace, I laughed and looked away. At the counter was a teen, practically salivating over his food. He was stuffing eggs into a wrapped waffle.

That's when the puzzle was revealed. At that moment I learned why I had the craving a few weeks earlier. The waffle looked just like the "waffle" cone pistachio ice cream. My brain associated the waffle cone with drug use because Waffle House is where I would smoke crack.

I'm always impressed with how our brain works. But I'm more interested in knowing about my addiction. Sometimes I'll know why I'm craving. Other times, I just won't. And I'm cool with that.

Instead of being fearful of cravings, I think we should access the situation. The bottom line for me is: do I have reservations? If my brain is making subconscious associations, then cool. But if I have reservations to use, I have to address that.

For some people, the "why" may not even be important. For me, it is. What's even more important is knowing we don't have to use behind a craving.

The Power of No

At this point in my life, I chose to deal with rigorous honesty. And honestly, there are days I want to use. That may sound crazy, especially because I'm writing a book about sober slogans. But it's not crazy, at all. Wanting to use and using, are two different things.

Not too long ago I gave up eating meat and poultry. I'm a typical guy, so I grew up on pizza and burgers. I really loved burgers. I was the guy who would eat five pounders. But today I'm pescatarian. I eat fruits, vegetables, and seafood.

I know eating meat isn't good for my health, so I don't indulge anymore. But that doesn't mean I don't crave it. Burgers are an American staple, so I'm bound to run into them. And I'm cool with that. More power to those who can still eat them. I can't, so I don't.

Since I'm an "all or nothing" kind of guy, I know that one's too many. If I eat a burger, I can throw being a pescatarian out of the window. That first burger will get the ball rolling. Let's not forget that I'm an addict. If I hit that resume button, it won't stop with just burgers.

My mind works like this: "*Now that I'm back eating burgers, I should eat beef, in general. As long as I'm eating beef, I should just start eating pork again, also. Now that I'm eating meat again, chicken and turkey is a given, since they're the lesser evils, anyway, right? And we can't stop there! I might as well start the chocolates again. Yeah, I should pick up a big bag of Hershey's Kisses at Kroger. Why did I ever want to be a pescatarian, anyway?*"

That's just the way my brain works. I'm an addict. But since I'm aware of this, I have power. I have the power to say no. So far, I've successfully used that power to not eat meat, even when I crave it. And I've also been successful with not relapsing.

So, there are times that I want to use, but I don't. Having those thoughts doesn't make me a bad person. Nor doesn't it make me a failed recovering addict. What I do with those thoughts is what counts.

I choose to say no, when I have those thoughts. I say no because I like being sober. I like waking up and posting my clean day on my Instagram. I like the chubby belly I have. I like sleeping indoors on a bed. I like thinking clearly. Most importantly, I like who I am becoming.

I express the power of "No," every time I say "Yes" to my sobriety. I have a saying that's gotten me this far. It's a saying that I love. "It's going to be alright, because it is alright."

By focusing on who I want to become, I am no longer who I don't want to be. I hope that doesn't sound like mumbo jumbo. I hope not. What I'm basically saying is, I am a recovering addict. By recovering who I was meant to be, I am no longer a "using" addict.

By focusing on being a pescatarian, I am no longer a meat eater. Saying no to eating meat and poultry, means I am saying yes to being a pescatarian. It's all about where my focus is. We grow in the areas where we place our focus.

Laws of Attraction

I used to focus on getting high. I'm an "all or nothing" kind of guy. Sometimes that has worked in my favor. In many cases, it hasn't. I've learned to use that aspect of my personality for sobriety. And I'm thankful for it. My daily focus is on being sober.

I'm also focusing on helping others stay clean. And you know what? By me helping others with their sobriety, I in turn help myself.

I have an app I use that tracks my clean days. Every day I post my clean day on Instagram and Facebook. It's not for clout. It's not for others to compliment me, although they do, and that's nice. But I post my clean time because it inspires me and holds me accountable. Daily reflections of my clean time keep me clean and sober.

I'm a strong believer in the 'Laws of Attraction.' I believe we attract two things in life: who we are and who we want to be. The philosophy of the 'Laws of Attraction' is quite simple. The more positivity you put into the universe, the more positivity you get. The opposite is also true.

When I focused on my addiction, it grew. The more drugs I did, the more I wanted. The more drugs I wanted, the more I received. Since we don't live life in a vacuum, my drug "lifestyle" included other people. Since I lived a lifestyle of drug use, that included meeting people who had the same lifestyle.

I attracted that kind of lifestyle because that's what I focused on. Today I'm sober, not just abstinent. The more sober I become, the more I live a sober lifestyle. For me that includes several things: the books I read, the people I socialize with, even the interests I have on social media.

Some people believe that "opposites attract." This is true for magnets, but not humans. Drug addicts attract the company of drug addicts. I've never seen recovering addicts hang out with users. They have two different focuses. When the "using" addict chooses to focus on recovery, they will attract sobriety. It's all about where we put our focus.

I've learned to focus on what I want, not what I don't want. I don't think about not relapsing. I focus on staying sober. This may sound like semantics to some, but not to me.

If I'm walking a path of recovery and living sober, I won't relapse. It's impossible to relapse when I focus on recovery. When I focus on staying clean, I don't worry about not being clean.

The more I focus on sobriety, the more I want it. I want to learn more about my disease, so that I can help others. I want to experience a sober life, so that I can inspire others.

I've been to meetings where the speaker says, "If I can do it, I know you can do it." I've heard that from several people. People from different meetings, who didn't know each other. But they knew themselves. They knew just how difficult it was for them to refocus. Each of those anonymous, recovering addicts shifted their focus. They gave up a lifestyle of drug use and embraced a lifestyle of sobriety.

Now I'm that guy. I'm the guy saying if I can do it, then I know you can also. I'm the guy who took over 30 years to get sober. I was a stubborn kid, who thought I knew it all. All I knew was the pain that was caused as a child. And for years I focused on that pain.

The day I chose to shift my focus, my new life began. Each day that I'm sober, I attract more energy to be sober. I attract the power to live another day in sobriety. I attract the power of sober friends. Some of these friends are on social media.

I tried to deal with my pain by abusing drugs and women. In the end, I abused myself the most. I repeated that cycle for three decades. Little did I know, I was giving power to past circumstances. Life moved on, but I didn't.

I had to shift my focus to the power within me. I have the power to attract positive energy in life. That positive energy is what will build me into a better me. As long as I focus on becoming a better me, I never have to worry about a relapse. My higher power will do the rest. The Laws of Attraction will do the rest.

My passion is to grow into a better version of me. I also have a passion to assist others with their growth. That is the purpose of this book series. There are spiritual principles behind our sober slogans. This is my way of saying thank you to those who coined these terms. I believe I'll be able to accomplish this because I'm sober. I also know I can only get there if I take it *one day at a time....*

One Day at A Time

"The future comes one day at a time..."

—Dean Acheson

Welcome to the Program

Everyone has their own road to recovery. Since no two people are the same, no one has the exact same transformation. And that is what it takes to get from addiction to sobriety—a transformation.

Many people—like myself—start off in treatment. Although I checked myself into a program, I hated institutions. After being in prison for so many years, I thought of all institutions as "jails."

But I knew I needed a program to help me think straight. No matter how much I disliked being there, that's exactly where I needed to be.

Quite honestly, my transformation occurred because of the folks at "The Crane." In hindsight, the program worked for me because of their "modality," or method of treatment. They have a "peer-delivered" approach.

I'm really big on a person's qualifications. Don't get me wrong, you can "learn" from just about anyone.

But when we're teaching someone how to stay clean, you have to have credentials.

In my book, there's no better credentials than actually being in recovery. I would much rather engage with a recovering addict of 20 years, than someone who just passed an exam. That's just my preference.

Once I realized the staff actually "lived" what they taught, my guard dropped. It took about a month before I started participating in group, though. But that was due to me not liking institutions, in general.

Trust the Process

While I was physically at the treatment facility, my mind was focused on trivial matters. I didn't like the Director or the staff at the residence. I didn't like the guys I lived with. In all reality, I didn't like being sober, yet. I wasn't used to it. I had a few months clean, but this was after a five-year binge.

Getting sober was a big step for me. Getting sober in a treatment program? That was difficult, to say the least.

I was still having a difficult time "letting go" of things. Anger fueled me for many years of my life. I was angry with my parents. I was angry with the justice system. I was angry with my ex-wife. Truthfully, I was angry with myself.

At first, I couldn't help comparing the program to prison. In prison, they give you a schedule to live by. There are limited choices in what "programs" you can participate in. Not much changes, except for those times when you get a visit. You wake up and go where you're told. You keep your head down and stay out of trouble. Do that, and your time will go smoothly.

I felt like the residence I lived in functioned the same way. They told us what time to get up and what to do. If we violated the rules, there were consequences. Some people received favoritism; others did not.

In treatment there's always a social justice type of guy. I played that part, at first. I knew how to run the program better than the director. My voice was a representation of the community. I spoke for those who didn't have the courage to speak for themselves.

My peers tolerated my rants. While I ran down a list of injustices, they would give each other the side eye. If you've been in any kind of institution, there's always that guy. Like I said, they tolerated me.

After a month, we started going to outside meetings. The Covid-19 numbers dropped, so the director allowed us social interaction. Prior to that we'd all sit in the dining room around a table and have meetings on Zoom. It was a miserable experience.

At the first meeting we attended, someone spoke about "trusting the process." It was exactly what I needed to hear. The speaker was a young woman, dressed in army fatigues. She had just come back from a relapse and was grateful for being alive. She poignantly explained how "staying in her head" led her to leaving the program too early. By not allowing herself enough time to "soak up the knowledge," she relapsed.

Watching the tough young woman pause to blow her nose, made me realize something. If I didn't change my attitude, I could possibly be next. As much as I complained, I knew I didn't want to relapse.

My speeches had nothing to do with our conditions. I was just miserable and having manic episodes. I feared recovery, but knew I needed it. By pointing the finger at everyone else, I wasn't focusing on myself. If I kept that up, my addiction would get the best of me.

The director of the program liked to remind us that we sought his help, not the other way around. And he was right. While I was in Dekalb Crisis Center, I filled out an application for My Brother's Keeper. They didn't call the crisis center looking for me.

After the meeting, I decided to accept my reality. I said I wanted to recover. I would have to trust the process. I would have to swallow my pride and follow the rules. If I could do ten years in prison, I could handle a six-month program.

I had a grown-up conversation with myself. I just had a five-year binge. How many times did I blindly trust people I didn't know? So, why wouldn't I want to trust a program that would help with my recovery? Weren't they referred by the crisis center? Didn't I ask them to accept me? Didn't I want to be sober?

Sometimes we have a moment of clarity that redirects our course. I made up my mind to keep my mouth shut. I made up my mind to become helpful in any way I could. If the front parking lot needed sweeping, I did it. If someone needed to cook for the house, I did it.

Being of service became more important than complaining. Being helpful shifted my attention. I was trusting the process. At first, I still griped inside, but I no longer made people listen to me. If someone asked how I was doing, I'd respond with something positive. I didn't feel all that positive, but I was trusting the process.

Until one day, I didn't need to pretend about my feelings. There wasn't a magic moment, or anything. I just woke up one day feeling grateful. During my "fake it until you make it" phase, I held on to gratitude. That's what got me through. I was trusting the process.

I still didn't like everyone or the way the program was ran. That really didn't change. But my focus changed. I was taking it one day at a time. By having that attitude, the path became clear to me.

I didn't have to "like" everyone in the program. I didn't have to "like" all the rules of the program. I just had to stay clean and follow the rules. It was as simple as that. As long as I stayed sober, life would get better. I would get better.

There were days my cravings made my body shake. There were nights I'd cry myself to sleep. Drug dreams, flashbacks, outbursts—I survived them all. Sometimes I shared what I was going through. Sometimes I didn't. But I was trusting the process.

I didn't want to be like the young woman in the army fatigues. I didn't want my addiction to trick me into leaving the program early. I knew what the streets had in store for me. I didn't want to gamble with my life anymore. No matter what I had to endure in the program, I knew it was better than being in the streets. I was trusting the process.

At Paula Crane we'd have group sessions. To start the sessions, we were asked to express our feelings, and how many clean days we had. Even though I was trusting the process, I'd tell them I didn't like being there. I'd also let them know I wasn't going anywhere. The staff would thank me for my honesty and encourage me to keep trusting the process. I did.

By doing so, my focus shifted from misery to acting grateful to being grateful. I can still remember Mr. Donald congratulating me. I woke up one day filled with gratitude. When it was my turn to "check in," I expressed that gratitude. I wasn't faking it anymore and it felt good.

There was a turning point for me, and I began to enjoy treatment. I gained perspective and needed to share about it. Treatment wasn't an institution, but a school. The focus of treatment is relapse prevention.

We were being bombarded with information overload. The hope is that we'd absorb critical tools and use them when we left. Everything they taught us was in preparation for when we left. Therapy sessions, group sessions, the skits—it was all to prepare us for the real world.

Once that clicked, I absorbed as much as I could. I trusted the process and was grateful for it.

The Day-by-Day Method

I used to get jealous of other people's clean time. I know that's immature, but it's true.

Before sobriety, I thought most people lied about their clean time. Sure, I knew there were some honest people out there. But I thought most of them were full of crap.

I projected my insecurities onto other people. There were days I wanted to be clean. I missed my children and missed feeling healthy. I wanted to look in the mirror and be proud of myself. But I didn't think I could do it. I wanted sobriety but didn't think I could attain it.

When I thought about my addictive past and unknown future, I'd get overwhelmed with fear. I'd ask myself if I could honestly live a life without drugs. For five years I didn't believe I could, so I kept using.

Sure, there are plenty of people who have more time than I do. And yes, I have more time than others. But at the end of the day, sobriety isn't about comparing clean time. Sobriety is about learning and applying spiritual principles. I've learned from those who have more time than I do. And I hope those with less time than mine, can learn from me.

I don't have yesterday because it's gone. I don't have tomorrow because it's not here, yet. But I do have today. I do have this beautiful sliver of time we call a Day, to make the choice to stay clean. And honestly, that's all I have. That's all any of us have, really.

Russell Brand's book, "Recovery: Freedom from Addiction," assisted me in a few ways. One major takeaway for me was the understanding that all I have is "today."

Russell says his sponsor explained to him that to achieve a year of sobriety, he had to focus on the day he had. And if he did that successfully, he would get a year clean. Then he'd get another year clean. But he would only get that year by taking it one day at a time. At the time of this writing, he has 17 years clean.

During his early stages of recovery, Russell struggled with anxiety from his fear of failure and the unknown. Just like many of us, he doubted whether he could seriously commit to a life without drug use. Once he understood the concept of sobriety on a day-by-day basis, he was able to move forward.

I wanted to grasp the concept, so I could also move forward. I admit, at first, viewing my life from a new perspective was aggravating. I was used to seeing myself as a drug addict.

When I thought about how I was going to spend my day, the answer was easy—numbing myself by using drugs. When I woke up, it was the first thing I thought about. If I had drugs, it was the first thing I did. When I thought about how I would spend the rest of my day, the answer was obvious. When I thought about what I'd be doing the next day—the answer was obvious.

When I found Russell's book, I was in Dekalb Crisis Center. I had a little clean time, but still had concerns about relapsing. I wasn't going to live the rest of my life at the crisis center. And although I was waiting for approval from a treatment program, I wasn't going to spend the rest of my life in there, either.

For me to live perpetually sober, I'd have to renew my viewpoint about time. The new concept of seeing myself sober in the future meant I had to see myself sober in every moment, but the most important moment was right now—and it would always be "right now."

I had to embrace what I coined, "The Day-by-Day Method." After reading what Russell Brand wrote on the subject, that's what my mind labeled it as. Recovering addicts with a lot of time basically all said this is how they achieved their sobriety.

If I wanted to live the rest of my life sober, I would have to do it "one day at a time." Sometimes it's easier for me to break down information, in order for me to understand better. So, that's what I did with this newfound concept.

If I wanted to be sober for a week, then for seven days I'd have to go without drugs. If I wanted that week of sobriety, I would have to claim victory— every single day, for seven consecutive days.

Maybe this is a simple concept for some, but it wasn't for me. I was used to giving in to the call of drugs. If I had an uncomfortable thought, that would lead to an uncomfortable feeling. I never wanted to feel anything, so I used. I was very aware about this aspect of my personality. I did not like to "feel."

I knew that I used because I didn't know how to deal with my emotions. I was what they call "emotionally immature." But if I could just learn to "deal" with my feelings, maybe I could stop using.

That's when I received clarity on what Russell Brand's sponsor meant by taking it "one day at a time."

That meant dealing with a lot of feelings, daily. If the past was gone and the future didn't exist, then all I had was the moment. If I could just deal with my feelings, in the moment, and allow them to pass, then I could get through each day, without using. I had a lot of work ahead.

Dealing with Our Emotions

The fear of having to deal with my feelings without drugs was overwhelming. But I knew that feelings pass. I also knew that there were times—during active addiction—that I "felt" like using but didn't.

Sometimes the feeling of shame was more potent than a craving. In those instances, even if I had drugs, I wouldn't use. One feeling had more power than another feeling.

If I could replace a craving, with a more powerful feeling, I would conquer that moment. I did it while I was using, even if it wasn't on purpose. Maybe if I learned how to force myself to do it, I'd get the answer.

A short while after reading about Russell's talk with his sponsor, I had an experience.

I was in the crisis center, feeling sorry for myself. If my mind wasn't occupied, I'd find ways to think negatively about myself. At the time, I was at a healthy weight. I wasn't skinny or malnourished. On this particular day, my mind didn't see it that way.

I kept telling myself that I was still underweight. The thought of it gripped me for most of the day. The more I thought about, the worse I felt. Once the feelings of shame kicked in, I wanted to use.

I hadn't had a craving in a few weeks, but I did that day. For most of the day, my brain played ping pong. I went back and forth, thinking about being malnourished, then wanting to use. Hours went by and I was stuck on the same two negative thoughts. Eventually I became mentally exhausted.

The thought of me being malnourished circled around again. That's when I jumped up from my bed and rushed to the bathroom. I wanted to see myself in the mirror.

Once I laid eyes on my round face, I was relieved. It looked like I gained weight. I still wasn't satisfied, so I asked a staff member for the scale. I definitely gained weight. I was a little more than 170lbs. I smiled and handed the scale back. I walked away thinking, "I look good up in here!"

It took most of the day, but as soon as I changed my thoughts, my feelings changed. As soon as I started to feel better about my weight, the cravings went away. I didn't even realize the cravings stopped until later than evening.

But I learned something that day. I learned that I needed to deal with my emotions. I knew I needed therapy, but I wasn't getting much of that at the crisis center. Until I did start therapy, the easiest

ONE DAY AT A TIME

way to deal with my emotions was to change my thoughts.

Since then, I did go through therapy. (Depending on who you ask, I still need a few sessions.) But what I learned that day at the crisis center is basically what I learned in therapy. By changing my thoughts, I could change my emotions.

The Power of Thought

There are moments in our lives when a simple truth changes everything. These truths can be delivered through intuition, our environment or from people.

I was blessed to meet someone who had a profound effect on my life.

From Dekalb Crisis Center, I went to My Brother's Keeper. Due to Covid-19 we had to have our sessions via Zoom meetings. I first met Ms. Angela Wilson onscreen. I had no idea, the no-nonsense woman with the colorful glasses, would be my counselor. Nor did I know she would plant a seed of hope and self-belief that would be crucial to my sobriety.

Having sessions with Ms. Angela always led back to the way I viewed myself. I honestly dreaded having sessions with her. I only felt this way because she made me look at myself. I didn't like myself very much, at the time.

What stuck to me was her message of self-belief. After one emotional session, it got me thinking. If I could change the way I viewed myself, who would I be?

Underneath my bravado and impressive vocabulary, I still looked at myself as a crackhead. Even with a few months clean, I still saw a crackhead looking back in the mirror.

I wouldn't survive when I left treatment, if that was what I saw. I was going to have to change that. So, I started watching YouTube videos about the power of thought. I watched videos from Deepak Chopra, Joe Dispenza, and others.

While watching one video, I recalled my experience at Dekalb Crisis Center. I heard something in the video that made me pause it, and vividly recollect my recent experience.

Back at Dekalb Crisis Center I was able to stop my craving when I changed my thought. I thought I was skinny. I related being skinny with smoking crack. That thought led to me feeling shame, which led to me having a craving. Once my thought changed about the way I viewed myself, my feelings changed. As a result, my cravings went away.

A few hours prior to watching the video, I had a session with Ms. Angela. After my recollection, a door opened in my mind.

For me to reframe my self-belief, I would have to start practicing new thoughts about myself. It was also imperative that I think about why I had my current belief system, in the first place.

What I've learned about the power of thought has enabled me to be sober. I no longer view myself as a crackhead. I no longer view myself as a victim, genetically predisposed to drug addiction. Yes, my family does have a history with drug and alcohol addiction. I can't discount that fact.

But I am not a victim of those past choices members of my family made. I am not a victim of the past choices I made. Today, I am something different.

Today I am a victor, not a victim. Every day I chose to see myself as a success story. In doing so, I have put this successful energy in motion.

Let me back up a bit. Let's go back to when I was still in the program. After watching videos about the power of thought, I'd think positively about my future. I'd say positive affirmations in the mirror, because Ms. Angela advised me to. But then I started doing some other things.

The more videos I watched about the power of thought, the more I learned. It wasn't enough to just have random positive thoughts throughout the day. If I was going to reframe the way I viewed myself, then I'd have to make it a habit to think positively.

So, I made it a habit to wake up every day and think positively. Of course, it took time to get into the habit, but once formed, it changed me. I made it a routine to do two things before I got out of bed. I still do it today:

Thoughts of Gratitude. The first thing I do when I wake up is say thank you to my Higher Power. Not too long ago I was homeless. Some nights I'd sleep in an abandoned building. Some nights I'd sleep on the roof. I even slept in burnt up, abandoned cars. These days I sleep on a comfy bed. I'm grateful. I'm grateful for the air-conditioned apartment, food in the fridge, and a loving woman I call my friend and partner. I don't get out of bed without a prayer of gratitude.

Thoughts of Self-belief. While still in the program, I conceived the thought to write this book. As fate would have it, within the first week of me leaving, I was able to start writing. Since the day I thought about the value "Sober Slogans" would bring to addicts, it became my passion. I've always known I could write a book. Now I have a reason to. I don't get out of bed without thinking about how to improve myself.

My self-belief has shifted from victim to victor. For over two decades I've said that I would write a book. Who would've known that as soon as I started focusing on that thought, my life would move in the direction of making it happen?

I am a sober enthusiast. I believe sobriety is so much more than not using. Essentially, my sobriety is rooted in thinking positive about myself.

Over the years I taught my brain to be my enemy. It is used to being off balance with drugs. It is used to having negative self-talk. What do you think is going to happen when you start redesigning your brain to be healthy? It's going to seek to function in the way it is used to.

I still have random thoughts about getting high. I also still have random flashbacks about getting high. In addition, I have random emotions associated with those thoughts. Random feelings of shame and guilt disrupt feelings of gratitude and pride.

Even while writing "Sober Slogans," I've had some battles. I'm not used to accomplishing my goals. I'm not used to thinking of other people; let alone bringing value to the lives of other addicts.

On several occasions, while writing a thought-provoking passage, I've had negative thoughts. I second-guess myself, a lot. I've told myself I don't have enough clean time to write this kind of material. I've told myself that I can't even write and I'm only fooling myself.

But I've made a lifetime commitment to not yield to my old way of thinking. So, I do what I must, in order to change negative thoughts into positive ones.

Sometimes that means looking at a funny video on Tik Tok. Sometimes that means visualizing a happy future. Then there are times I just have to cry. Sometimes alone, sometimes in my partner's lap while she strokes my bald head. But I change those negative thoughts into positive ones.

Your methods are sure to be different from mine. You may not even have a bald head. But you get the point. We do what we must, in order to shift that negative to a positive.

There are going to be days when our emotions go haywire. It doesn't matter how much clean time we achieve. We're addicts, so our brain needs constant rewiring. Random thoughts will trigger random emotions. We just have to deal with them.

I think, like everything else that's worth our attention, it takes practice. Like the bodybuilder, who trains daily, we have to do the same with positive thinking. Rigorously training our brain to reflect positive thoughts will yield an improved self-image.

From Daydreaming to Visualizing

Self-worth and self-belief were foreign concepts to me as a child. In reality, I hated myself, so I couldn't see myself being successful. I just wanted my life to have meaning. I wanted to feel loved by someone. Up until the age of 15 I'd mentally whisk myself away. Then I started letting the drugs do it for me.

As a teen I'd say, "I'm gonna be a...." My so-called dreams would switch up all the time. I was the guy who lied about what I had going on. If there was a new trend, I'd claim some kind of stake in it, to impress people. I was going to be a rapper, a songwriter, a filmmaker. Yeah, sure I was.

I can still remember a girl from my projects saying, "Jeff, stop beating me in the head." It was the first time I ever heard the term, but I knew exactly what she meant.

Everyone from my projects knew I was a crack addict. They all knew me to spin a story. I didn't work. I dropped out of high school. I smoked crack. I was just a dreamer. A loser. A scrub.

Funny thing though, these days I still dream. But I do it with a purpose and then follow up with action. Guess you can say I'm a dream-chaser.

Today my daydreaming has evolved into something much more sophisticated. Now I do what successful people call 'visualize.' When you visualize, you form a mental image of an object or event. I focus on events, not so much objects. Those events include me being successful with various endeavors.

This may sound far-fetched, but what I'm about to tell you is the truth. Toward the last year of my relapse-binge, I envisioned myself as a successful writer. I was still getting high, but I would watch motivational videos.

When I wasn't using, I'd watch videos from Les Brown, Evan Carmichael, and Eric Thomas. Their message of hope and self-love planted a seed in my heart. (A few years later, this seed was fertilized by Ms. Angela.)

I didn't have a plan nor much belief in myself. But I exposed myself to content that would form a basis for change. And the biggest action on my part was "seeing" a better version of myself. Although I had no idea how I would do it, I visualized myself as a successful writer.

The Power of Visualization

When Kanye West explained the power of visualization, it touched me. Prior to watching his video, I heard the term. However, when he explained it, I "felt" it.

Before he was the icon we all know him as—he saw it in his dreams. Kanye would even "act" out scenarios when no one was around!

While making beats that only a handful of people knew about—he believed himself to be, "the Savior of Chicago."

Kanye said he envisioned himself being friends with Jay-Z and Diddy. He visualized himself at parties, hanging out with the elite superstars of Hip-Hop. He visualized those same superstars loving his music. The guy even had the audacity to visualize himself as a legend!

He did this while perfecting his craft at his mother's house. He saw his dreams, as a reality, years before they came true. More importantly, he did it every day, until those dreams became a reality.

I figured if it could work for Kanye, it could work for me. Even in the midst of spiritual darkness, I'd visualize a better me. I did it when I was abstinent. I even did it when I was high on crack.

I knew it was a longshot, but I keep thinking that one day I'd get sober. Deep inside my gut, I knew I could be a better person. Underneath all the pain I felt, there was something there.

I wasn't daydreaming any longer. I was pulling in the energy of a better life. I was pulling in the energy of a better me. This might sound foolish, but it worked. I saw myself sober, writing a book. Today I am living out that visualization. Today, as I write this, I am a living example of the power of visualization. If it worked for Kayne and worked for me—I know it can work for you.

Visualize then Actualize

Have you ever heard R. Kelly's song, "I believe I can fly"? It's in the movie "Space Jam," with Michael Jordan and Bugs Bunny. That song is powerful. I suggest you listen to it if you haven't. Even if you have heard it, listen to it again.

The song is about manifesting your dreams. It's about believing in yourself, even when your circumstances are bleak. I'm speaking from a place of experience here. I was down. I was down bad.

I can remember smoking crack, crying to myself, while listening to R. Kelly. Although I chose that life, I did so because I didn't believe I could do better. I didn't believe in myself.

But under the pain, I yearned for better. Under the pain, I knew that if I could just find the courage—I could make it. I knew that if I could just claw my way from under the dirt, I could get back to the living.

Since getting sober, I still visualize. I had to visualize the action, until I actualized the vision.

Each step on my journey, I visualize going further. When I was in treatment, I would visualize myself writing. I'd sit on the edge of my bed, close my eyes, and pretend to type. I didn't have a laptop then. But that didn't matter. What mattered was, I knew I would have a laptop, one day. What mattered was, I knew that as long as I continued "seeing" myself as a writer, I would become a writer. I knew that if I stayed true my vision, it would become a reality.

I knew that through visualizing I was sober. I believed if it worked to get me that far, then it should work to get me further. So far, my theory is correct. I am living what I visualized.

Months ago, I sat on the edge of a bed, focusing my energy on my future. Today, literally as I write this, I am living that future. That is the power of visualization. That is the power of believing in yourself.

Now, it's a part of my daily routine. Every morning I have a cup of coffee and look at the skyline. My partner and I want to move to Maine one day. So, while I sip my coffee, I envision a lighthouse next to a cove where people are parasailing.

So far, my visualization has been actualized by getting sober and writing a book. I'm sure one day I'll be skipping pebbles on the beach in Portland. I can see it. I believe it. So, I will achieve it.

Envision your Triggers

The more I learn about a subject, the more I want to learn about it. I've always been that way. I love learning. Once I experienced the power of visualization, I delved further.

Motivational videos helped plant a seed in me. My path to visualizing came from watching Kayne West in a motivational video. I'm a believer in the concept "if it ain't broke, don't fix it." So, I still watch videos about motivation. And I still watch videos about visualization.

Brendon Burchard is a New York Times bestseller. He writes books about leadership and business. I learned about him by watching a motivational video on Evan Carmichael's YouTube channel. What this man shared about visualization has changed my life.

Prior to watching Brendon's video, I only visualized about my successes. When I visualized my writing career, I only focused on the positives. I would see myself writing the book. Then I'd focus on having the book in my hand. I'd see my readers leaving comments on Amazon. Then I'd see the speaking engagements that are sure to come. Do you see the pattern here? Everything I focused on were wins. Just the positives. Just the successes. But life doesn't work like that, now does it?

Not once did I envision "writer's block." Not once did I envision moments of self-doubt. Or writing in flurries, only to delete my work out of frustration. Although this is my first book, I've written before. I've experienced all three of these occurrences in the past. Yet, I didn't envision them. I focused on the upsides of my endeavors. But not the downsides.

At first, it may seem illogical to visualize failure. Why would I purposely "see" myself lose? But that's not what I'm suggesting. What I am suggesting is that we envision the struggles—not the failures—of our endeavors. I learned this from Brendon Burchard.

Let us talk about my visualization routines centered around sobriety. When I first started with the process, I'd focus on the happy times. I'd see myself holding sobriety coins and smiling. I'd focus on the emotions of my success. I'd see all of my friends giving me pats on the back. You know, all the good stuff.

But I never envisioned myself in an argument with my partner. I didn't see myself waking up from a drug dream. Or having butterflies in my stomach from driving through an old neighborhood.

These are all triggers. These are examples of real-life struggles that we must conquer. But I didn't envision them. I didn't envision my triggers.

Mr. Burchard advises that we intentionally focus on our struggles. Conquering pressures is a natural part of any successful endeavor. Internal and external struggles must be conquered daily.

When we're not visualizing, we have to perform actions that will lead to our desired results. If I know that triggers are a part of the process, not visualizing them does me a disservice.

Let's take the example of driving through an old neighborhood. If I drive down Memorial Drive in Atlanta, I'm going to feel a lot of emotions. That was my stomping ground.

So, once my brain recognizes familiar images, I'll have familiar emotions. I'm going to experience fear, and anxiety. And I'm going to get a craving. If I give in to those cravings, I'll relapse.

Let's say I visualized this situation in preparation for the event. I should "see" myself conquering the emotions of fear and anxiety. I should "see" myself conquering the craving.

By doing so, I'm rewiring my brain and emotions. The purpose of this particular visualization is to conquer the struggle. So, we must include the process of overcoming the struggle when we visualize.

So, the next time I'm in that neighborhood, my reaction should be different. Instead of feeling anxiety and fear, something else should occur. I should anticipate feeling relief, pride, and a sense of gratitude.

Of course, this takes practice. It takes time to rewire the brain. But if we make it a routine, we'll build the memory muscles of our brain and body.

Look at it like you're mentally preparing yourself for the inevitable. Making this a daily habit, one day at a time, will align you with a successful future. I'm living proof that this is possible.

Being Grateful

I don't know your story. But I do know if you're reading this book, you have a desire. You have a desire to become a better you. I applaud you for that.

If you didn't use today, I applaud you. If you didn't use within the last few minutes, I applaud you. Every moment you choose to improve yourself should be applauded. Every time you do something to become better, you should applaud yourself.

I say this because I know the struggle. I'm a recovering addict, but I'm still an addict. The greatest battle exists within our own minds. How we view ourselves, our negative self-talk. We're our own worst enemy. This is our struggle. But I'm learning to be my own best friend.

I'm learning that in order to do this, I must recover. I must recover on a daily basis. I must recover one day at a time. And I must do this for the rest of my life.

Sure, there are battles ahead. I've already conquered a few. But there are a lot more in front of me. Now that I'm recovering, I welcome those battles. Now that I'm recovering, I need those battles.

I'm honestly proud of the man I am today. I wake up feeling gratitude. I'm grateful that I listened to my Higher Power. I'm grateful that I gave myself a chance. I'm grateful that I'm alive and healthy. I'm grateful that my partner is also my friend. I'm grateful that I've learned to be a friend to myself.

But I'm only sober because I pushed through my fears. And let's face it, it's scary. Recovery is scary. It's difficult retraining how we view ourselves. We've been beating ourselves up for a long time. I was a crackhead for a long time.

Now I'm a recovering addict. Now I'm a writer. One day I'll be a public speaker. One day I'll be a scriptwriter. And guess what? I'm grateful for what I've accomplished to get here. I'm even grateful for the goals I will accomplish in the future.

Never forget where you came from. Be grateful for the struggle. Be grateful for saying no to a craving. Be grateful for replacing negative self-talk with positive affirmations.

Embrace every win! Be grateful for who you are today. Be grateful for what you're about to achieve. Embrace the feeling now, because if you can believe it, you can achieve it. But you can only do that by working on yourself one day at a time.

So, who's up for a meeting....

90 Meetings In 90 Days

"The key to success is consistency."

—Zak Frazer

Advice for the Newcomer

It's advised that the newcomer-in-recovery go to 90 meetings in 90 days. At first, I couldn't see the logic. Honestly, I didn't want to see it. I didn't want to admit I NEEDED recovery. I already knew that I was an addict but didn't want to live "in the rooms." I didn't like myself, and didn't like other addicts, especially "recovering" addicts. That changed.

I can't stress enough that recovery is a spiritually based program. Once I accepted this and who I was, I was able to reinvent who I wanted to be.

Journey through Faith

I've been on a spiritual journey for some time now. Actually, I've been on one since the day I was born. I'm of the belief that I am a spiritual being, living out a human experience.

During my journey I've practiced several faiths. I've been a Christian, Sunni Muslim, and Five Percenter. My ex-wife practiced Christianity as a religion but grew up orthodox Jew. Her mother is 100% Jewish by faith and ethnicity. It's been interesting learning worldviews, histories, and practices. I've been blessed to have had this religious background.

These days I don't subscribe to any religion, but still respect them all. I do believe in a "higher power," though. And I believe we are all made in the image of this higher power. If I had to identify with any one religion at this point in my life, it would be the religion of LOVE.

Here's a funny story about my first A.A. meeting ever, when I was a Five Percenter...

The Defiant Teen

After two years in prison, I was paroled. Since I had a drug possession charge, I was mandated to go to "drug" meetings. In 1992 I attended my first A.A. meeting.

I was a very rebellious, misguided, nineteen-year-old. In addition to seeing life through a very narrow filter, I thought my drug addiction was a thing of the past.

At the time I was a member of 'The Five Percent Nation of Gods and Earths'. It's an off shoot of "The Nation of Islam," which is a black nationalist religion. We believed the black man is God, in the flesh.

There I was, a snotty nosed kid, full of denial, and angry with the world. Armed with a god-complex, and suffering from authority issues, I sneered at the predominantly white audience. My first meeting just HAD to be on step 3:

"We made a decision to turn our will and our lives over to the care of God *as we understood Him.*"

I was immediately put off when I heard the word "god." Without thinking, I jumped up and said the black man is god, and I didn't believe in this "Mystery God." My fists did a lot of punctuating and my Timberland boots stomped the dirty linoleum floor. I can only imagine how ridiculous I looked, with my bad acne, standing in my B-boy stance.

Ready for a debate, I stood on my "square," daring anyone to challenge me. My young mind reverted to prison. While in prison I debated with Muslims and Christians about the validity of a "Mystery God."

Me and my fellow believers lived by a few precepts:

1. The black man is God

2. All "religious" gods were "Mystery Gods"

3. All religions were societal constructs built to control the masses

After my outburst, I stood in silence, staring at a bunch of very confused recovering alcoholics. Although my physical disposition was aggressive, I just wanted to debate. Back in prison debating was fun. Those debates gave me an opportunity to show off my intellect. They made me feel relevant. At that moment, at my first A.A. meeting, I needed to feel relevant.

68

The speaker of the meeting was a much older man. Initially he was startled by my outburst, but quickly realized my level of immaturity. He didn't give me a chance to flex my pseudo-intellect.

In a respectful monotone he guided me back to Step 3. He asked that I read it aloud. I was still in debate-mode, so I took his request as a challenge. I figured he was using the material as a basis for a starting point in which to argue. Little did I know, he wouldn't give me a chance to disrupt the meeting any further.

I read Step 3 with much bravado. My plan was to breeze through the step in a respectful, non-threatening voice, then double back and go all Malcolm X on him. But dude wasn't having it.

As soon as I finished, he interjected and asked that I read the last four words. With a smirk on my face, I drawled, "*as we understood Him.*" At this point, the room calmed down a bit. I read the four words and was cut off in mid breath. His next move crushed me.

He explained that it was evident that I believed I was god, and that everyone in the meeting was cool with that assertion. (I looked around the room to see some people shake their heads in agreement.) He went on to inform me that since I was God, then I *knew* he had to sign my paperwork. Very sternly he explained if I didn't let them have a peaceful meeting, he wouldn't sign the papers. The blood drained from my face. Before I could respond, he called on someone who didn't even have their hand up. I pouted for the remainder of the meeting.

No one cared that I thought I was God. Being a spiritually based organization means "everyone's" understanding of God is valid.

"God" in Recovery

What I appreciate about A.A. and N.A. is there's no religious specificity. "God" in recovery is used as a universal term for people of all faiths, in addition to those without religious affiliation.

Go to enough meetings and you're bound to meet the following: atheists, agnostics, polytheists, Christians, Muslims, Hindus, Wiccans, and Jews.

If a Muslim calls God "Allah," and a Christian calls God "Jesus," it doesn't hinder the progress of the person who calls their God "Yahweh." That's the beauty of recovery. That's the beauty of the literature written around spiritual principles. The generic term "God" shows respect for all addicts, regardless of our religion, or the lack of a religion.

I've been to meetings where they use the term "God" interchangeably with the term, "Higher Power." I actually like both terms and have no issue with either. I've heard people balk at the word "God," but not at the term "Higher Power."

There are historical nuances with the word "God" whereas "Higher Power" really doesn't have a bad rap with addicts. I think it's more digestible.

Regardless which term you're comfortable with, in recovery "God" and "Higher Power" basically mean, "a power greater than you" or "me," for that matter.

No man is an Island

Maybe you've heard this quote before. Maybe not. I love it though. It's a portion of the famous quote from poet John Donne. The full quote, which actually comes from an essay, is as follows: **"No man is an island, entire of itself; every man is a piece of the continent."** I love this quote. It's been around since the 17th century for a reason.

The metaphor implies humans need to connect. It implies that yes, we are individuals—with our own lives—but we need social interaction, in order to thrive.

At the age of 19, I believed myself to be 'god in the flesh.' Still and all, I had to know my lessons and prove my knowledge, amongst other 'gods.' I had to connect with the other 'gods.' Even the mythological deities of Egyptian and Greek pantheons had social structures.

Various studies have shown that the human connection is as essential to our existence as food and water. Without getting scientific, I think we can agree that we are 'social creatures.'

Social media has given the world an opportunity to connect with like-minded people. Facebook, Instagram, and Tik Tok, are companies who have figured out how to monetize from our need to connect. I have profiles on Facebook and Instagram. I use Facebook and Instagram to socialize professionally and personally. I don't "do" Tik Toks, but I enjoy the platform.

If I'm in my comfort zone, I'm a silly guy. I enjoy laughter and making my loved ones laugh. (Just ask my partner, "Sassy," I'm a riot.) I've been diagnosed bi-polar, so there are days my mood swings a bit. It's not as bad as it used to be since I'm not using or drinking. But there are times when I just need a "pick me up."

So, what do I do these days to get that shot of endorphins, if I'm feeling down? I open up my Tik Tok app. Since laughter releases endorphins, which are "feel good" chemicals, I hit up Tik Tok for a few minutes. This company serves a few social groups, but I use it for the funnies. Follow Will Smith and Jason Derulo to see what I mean.

We all have a social gauge. Depending on our mood and the circumstances, that "gauge" will move. Generally, we are either an extrovert, or an introvert. Extroverts generally like to be around people. Introverts generally like to be by themselves. I've met extroverts, introverts, and a combination of both.

I'm primarily an introvert, believe it or not. I would much rather rent a movie on Amazon Prime, than sit in a theatre. I'm more comfortable buying a download, than attending a concert. Having said that, I do thrive in the right social environment. In the right environment, I'm the "life" of the party. Depending on my mood, and the context of the situation, I adapt. So, I'm what they call an "ambivert." (I'm a complex person, and always have been.) But I'm not alone.

A Place for Everyone

In the rooms of recovery, there is a 'place' for everyone. Ambivert, introvert, and extrovert. Alcoholic. Sexaholic. Cocaine addict. Whatever your addiction and personality, you'll be able to find a meeting. So, if you're an introverted alcoholic, you can hit an A.A. meeting and just "listen." You won't be forced to speak. No pressure. If you're an extroverted cocaine addict, you can grab an N.A. meeting and volunteer to read literature. And we already know there's no religious discrimination.

Now during the pandemic, we can also grab a Zoom meeting. Zoom meetings have actually made it even easier to network. I love that. It doesn't matter what time of day it is, there's a meeting. It doesn't even matter what state you live in. I'm from New York, but I live in Atlanta. I really enjoy being able to log into meetings in New York. Listening to a Puerto Rican from the Bronx talk about recovery is inspiring!

My Recovery Priority System

My mother and I haven't always seen eye to eye. We both have strong personalities. But I love and honor her. The woman is closing in on 20 years clean and sober! These days we network more than we used to. When you've been sober for some time, you basically design a blueprint for success.

If I had to prioritize how she's stayed clean, it would look like this:

1. Thank your Higher Power—Daily

2. Don't use—Ever

3. Network Regularly—meetings and
   socializing

I can't recall her breaking it down verbatim like this,
but I think I'm on point. I've personally adopted this
recovery priority system. I think it's a very logical
approach to staying clean. Every day I thank my
Higher Power for giving me life. Every day I hold
myself accountable and no matter what, I don't use.
And I regularly network with people in recovery. It's
working for me.

Why we Network

I use Tik Tok—which is a social platform—to get a
laugh, here and there. I use meetings—which are
social groups—to stay connected with other
recovering addicts.

Not networking with other addicts is a set-up for a
relapse. If we are of the same opinion that no man is
an island, then the same holds true for recovery. No
recovering addict can recover alone. Why would we
want to? We NEED each other!

Having access to people with similar struggles is a
blessing. Having access to people who have gone
through that struggle and triumphed?
Immeasurable blessings.

In recovery, we go to meetings to receive wisdom and
network. For me, going to a meeting is like attending

a free Masterclass. A Masterclass is a class taught by a prominent leader in their field.

If Spike Lee were doing a free Masterclass, I'd break my neck to attend. Why? Because I love scriptwriting. And because it's Spike "Mookie" Lee, so I would do the right thing. I'd attend that Masterclass for the wisdom and networking opportunities.

Speaking with my mother is a free Masterclass! Networking with my mother keeps me on track. If I'm going through something, she can reach into her memory bank and pull out an anecdote. She can do this, easy-peasy. With close to 20 years, she's learned a thing or two about how to apply the spiritual principles to her life. She's a source I trust.

Not everyone is blessed to have a mother in this position. Ok, but guess what? If you network, you're bound to hear that same kind of wisdom. Why? Because women like my mother are in the rooms. Men, with clean time like my mother, are in the rooms. The same kind of wisdom I get from her, is accessible in the rooms. So, aside from bragging on my moms, what am I really saying?

The Power of Networking

There is power in networking. No matter what your interest is, networking empowers you with education. When like-minded people connect, it's an enriching experience. Why? Because knowledge is power.

Social media has made connecting and engaging with like-minded people commonplace. Just think about Facebook "groups." Whatever you're interested in, I'm sure you can find it on Facebook. I'm currently in 12 Facebook groups. Some are for indie publishing, while others are for spirituality. I'm even in a few for pescatarian recipes. In each group I have an opportunity to learn more about my interests.

The reason we join groups is the learn. Whether you just scroll the posts or engage in the community, you're there to learn. Having the knowledge of others at your disposal is priceless.

Something cool happened in one of the Facebook groups I'm in. After asking for references for professional book cover designers, I was inundated with responses. These answers came from "published" authors. Authors who already have successful books on Amazon. Their selflessness was very humbling. I gained tons of knowledge and saved hours of time on research. The designer of this book's cover was actually a reference from that query. That's empowering!

When we go to meetings, we have the same opportunities. Recovery meetings are essentially "groups" of like-minded people. With five people in a meeting, your knowledge about sobriety will increase. With 30 people in a meeting? Your knowledge increases exponentially. And why exactly do we go to meetings, if not to learn how to live a life of sobriety?

Three Groups in One

Here's something interesting. Within every meeting you will find three levels of clean time.

In essence there are three groups within the big group:

1. Newcomers

2. One Year or Less

3. Multiple Years

Whether it's an in-person or Zoom meeting, you'll find the same dynamics. These three groups represent different stages of clean time:

Newcomers. Hearing from the newcomer reminds us that it's still hell out there. Newcomers provide a current perspective. They're like the new players in an old, twisted game. They provide up-to-date tales of a classic tragedy. Skip the phone. Skip the TV. Just listen to the newcomers. I promise you, aint no love in those streets. That was the case in 1989 when I started getting high. And it's still the case 32 years later. No one has to relapse to find that out. Pay attention when the newcomer speaks.

One Year or Less. Most people in their first year are in some form of treatment. Most don't make it. Within the first year of recovery, it's all about rewiring the brain. Learning new perspectives; starting new habits. Listening to people at this stage of recovery is a must. You'll hear about their struggles with self-acceptance, powerlessness, nightmares, relearning social skills and so much more. The two areas I struggled with the most were: self-belief and allowing myself to "feel." That first year is like boot-camp. But the ones who survive, have a solid foundation.

Multiple Years. Having just one day of clean time is a major success. But having a year or more is a phenomenal accomplishment! Everyone's journey is different. Some people went to treatment and some didn't. Regardless of the road taken, there are three things these people have in common. Each person goes to meetings, networks with other addicts, and has a sponsor. If you want to learn how to deal with life on life's terms—listen to these people! These people are like sages!

These are the three smaller groups in any meeting. Whatever stage of clean time you're in, you will be able to identify with someone. The newcomer will meet other scared, struggling addicts with knots in their stomach. Those close to a year will meet other frustrated addicts, who are learning how to live a sober life. And those with multiple years will meet others with an appreciation for recovery. Throw all of them in a room together for an hour and you get a spiritual expedition!

The Emotional Cycle

I'm not saying I've been to 100s of anniversary meetings. I've been to a few. By the time you get to one year clean, you'll be asked to speak or "share." It's about one addict helping another. It's about sharing the wisdom you've gained with other recovering addicts.

One thing I'm good at it is picking up on patterns in human behavior. And every single person I've heard share, basically said the same thing. After a year, every addict realized they went through a 'emotional cycle' when it came to their attitudes about meetings.

It didn't matter if it was an A.A. or N.A. meeting. It didn't matter if that person was an ambivert, introvert or extrovert. The cycle of emotions toward meetings was the same. They went from distain to acceptance to appreciation.

I went through the same cycle. My mother went through the same cycle. If you have a year or more, I'd like you to be honest and ask yourself if the same is true. Here's what I experienced and learned from others:

- **Distain.** I don't know about you but even after I decided to get sober, I was angry. I didn't like myself at the time and I didn't like people. I didn't want to accept that I needed recovery. Last thing I wanted to do was be around other addicts. I didn't have the patience to hear people 'ranting.' Ranting about this. Ranting about that. Just ranting. I wanted to get high but knew I couldn't. I believed most of the people in there wanted to get high, too. That's probably why they were ranting all the time.

- **Acceptance.** Eventually I got past my anger. I accepted my reality. I finally realized that I NEEDED recovery. I NEEDED to surround myself with people just like me. I NEEDED meetings since this is where "my" people were. I still didn't like the rantings. But when people shared, I heard my story. Most times it didn't sit well with me. I was being reminded of the guy I became, of the people I hurt. And I didn't like that. But I kept going to meetings.

- **Appreciation.** Eventually I became comfortable with my reality. I was an addict. It was in my genes. Addictive behaviors permeated my life. I started to envision a better me. I saw the value of meetings. People weren't ranting but sharing their unique experiences. These people were just like me, new 'creations' learning how to navigate a sober life. Recovering addicts became my champions, my new heroes.

I don't have as much time as some, but I do have more time than others. It's a process. But hands down, this is the emotional cycle people go through when it comes to their attitude toward meetings. Get enough meetings under your belt and you'll reach the 'appreciation' stage.

The 21/90 Rule

At the beginning of this chapter, I shared an experience. It was my very first A.A. meeting. That meeting became my home group because it was convenient for me. I was only going to meetings because I was on parole. One of the issues I had was going to 90 meetings in 90 days. I couldn't understand why A.A. members were so intense. My parole officer enforced this absurd requirement on me. I asked him what was the purpose of all this '90 in 90.' Dude wasn't one for much explaining. He kindly informed me the purpose for "me" was to avoid a parole violation.

Luckily not every newcomer is mandated to attend meetings. But there is validity in getting those 90 meetings in 90 days. I still haven't found out when A.A. or N.A. officially incorporated this, but I did find out something interesting.

Back in 1960 cosmetic surgeon, Dr. Maxwell Maltz wrote a self-help book, "Psycho Cybernetics: A New Way to Get More Living Out of Life." If you've ever heard of the "21/90 rule," this is where it comes from. Dr. Maltz asserted that if you commit to a personal or professional goal for 21 days, it will form a habit. He also believed after the three weeks, if you continued that habit for an entire 90 days, it would become a permanent lifestyle choice.

100-Day Challenges

Research varies, but I've found this is more or less accurate. Just look on social media. One popular trend is the "100-day challenge." Why not the "90-day" challenge? I have no idea. But if you can repeat an action for 90 days, then you can do it for 100 days. (If you're a recovering addict, read that last sentence over and think about this applied to your active addiction.)

I'm not sure who started the trend or when it started, but I like it. After watching a friend of mine post his "100 push-ups in 100-days" challenge, I was inspired. I wanted to begin an exercise regimen for 2021, so I challenged myself. I needed to ease back into the gym, so I hit the treadmill. Ultimately, I wanted to train for a 5k run. So, for 100 days I posted my progress on Instagram. Hitting the gym for 100 consecutive days, turned exercising into a permanent lifestyle choice.

90 in 90

So, does it make sense to attend 90 meetings in 90 days? I think so. Think about the benefits you get by socializing with other addicts. Think about the networking opportunities. Think about the spiritual wisdom. Let's be honest, the first 90 days are the hardest. Who can't use that added support from someone who has been in your exact shoes?

With every single meeting you're able to learn from multiple groups, at different stages in their recovery. If you're a newcomer, you have your peers and those with more wisdom. If you're within your first year, you have your peers, you can empathize with the newcomer, and learn from the veterans. If you're a seasoned recovering addict, you have your peers, and can share wisdom with those with less time. Everybody wins, every single time.

Make it a habit to do 90 meetings in 90 days. By the 3-month benchmark, meetings will be a lifestyle choice. And what is recovery, if not a lifestyle? What is sobriety, if not a lifestyle?

By 90 days, it won't be such a struggle. For some, it may still be. We all recover at our own rate. You may still distain meetings. Nothing's wrong with that. Just keep going to them. Eventually you'll accept your need for them. Then you'll appreciate meetings. That's a promise.

Keep going to meetings. That's where the power is. The spiritual power of one addict helping another. One day you'll find a home group. There you'll meet other addicts and enjoy years of sober friendships.

When I was using, I'd frequent the same crack dens. I'd see the same people because we went there to do the same things. Well, now that I'm in recovery I frequent places where there are recovering addicts. I go to where there are people doing the same things. Those people are going to meetings. It might be in a school. It might be in a church. It might be on a Zoom meeting. It really doesn't matter. What matters is there are other recovering addicts there, just like me.

Get Ready

After the 90 meetings, it ain't over. Oh, did you think it was over? That's just the start. You're just starting your life of sobriety. You're just starting your road to recovery.

You're just starting to redefine who you are. And what an amazing someone you are. Think of all the dreams you have. Now is the time those dreams can come true. Now is the time for you to start training yourself to be the best version you can possibly be.

Some people get into the mindset that sobriety isn't cool, that it's not fun. Please don't believe that. We're sober now, so life should be fun. Let me tell you what was not fun....

Getting chased by the police. Watching someone overdose. Contemplating suicide, every day. Getting chased by drug dealers. Having children talk disrespectful to me. Avoiding video chats. Getting chased by security guards. Feeling exhausted but having to sooth a craving. Sleeping in dumpsters. Getting chased by children. Having a heartbeat over 125. Watching prepubescent girls selling themselves. Getting chased.

Not only is sobriety cool, but it's also fascinating. Let me tell you why it's so cool...

We get to talk to others who share our struggle. We get to become friends with people who share our struggle. We can make our dreams come true. We get to beat the odds. We can feel proud of ourselves. We get to work on the issues that kept us back. We can inspire others with common struggles. We can make our dreams come true. We can hold a job. We can start a business. We can support our family. We can make our dreams come true. We can become whoever we want to be. We can make our dreams come true.

I don't know about you, but I think all of that is cool. I especially think it's cool that we can make our dreams come true. I say that because nothing is impossible when we're sober. But nothing is possible when we're using.

Get ready. Get ready for miracles to start happening. Get ready to start receiving blessings. Get ready to get to know you. What a wonderful you, you are. Get ready to start setting yourself up for success. Get ready to start learning. Get ready to start teaching. Get ready to be better. A better version of yourself. A version you could not imagine when you were using.

90 meetings is just the beginning. 90 meetings doesn't even scratch the surface. I'm not just talking about meetings in a room. I'm not just talking about meetings with other addicts. I'm talking about meetings with yourself. I'm talking about meetings with strangers, who become mentors. Meetings with motivational videos. Meetings with the gym. Meetings with motivational books. Meetings with nature.

I believe it's going to happen for you. I believe that with all of my heart. If you have taken the time to read this, then I know you are on your way. Anytime we choose to acquire knowledge that will improve us, we're on our way. You could be doing anything right now, but you're feeding your soul.

Get ready because life is about to change. As long as you stay focused, life is about to change. As long as you remain passionate about improving yourself, life is about to change. As long as you want that as much as you want to breathe, life is about to change.

On this road, we meet people who inspire us. We also meet people who get on our nerves. We're recovering addicts, so we're all still growing. What's important is that we put *principles before personalities....*

Principles Before Personalities

"Don't judge a book by its cover."

—English idiom

Having Perspective

A few years ago I used a sober living community as a pit-stop. I had no intention on getting sober. I just wanted to dry out for a few weeks. I only lasted a week, if that.

It was the only time I purposely "used" a sober community for selfish reasons. My stay was short, but I met two men who were instrumental to my growth: Josh, who became my sponsor for a week, and Fitzgerald.

Fitzgerald was the senior man of my housing unit. I honestly can't remember how many men lived there. Maybe four. Maybe ten. It was Fitzgerald's responsibility to make sure we were responsible. The man was serious about his responsibilities and his recovery.

Most of the guys didn't care for him. A few did, but not many. He was direct and intense. He'd also call you out, if he felt you weren't serious about recovery. His candor irked me. I can remember thinking, "What's up with this dude's energy?"

I didn't like his "energy" because I hadn't attained sobriety, yet. Fitzgerald was in recovery. I was playing the system. I was there for the freebies. He was there for the freedom sobriety gave him. I was using the community as a pit-stop. He was using it as a resource, on his road to recovery. Of course, our "energies" weren't aligned.

When I left the community, we'd still see each other. It was difficult not to bump into each other, since I was getting high right in back of his homegroup.

He wasn't surprised that I relapsed and had no problem telling me. I had no problem ignoring him. Although, there were a few times I let him say his piece. A part of me still wanted to hear "the message." But another part wanted to spite him. I'd watch his lips move and tune him out, while playing with the drugs in my pocket.

A few months after I left the program, I "tried" sobriety for a girlfriend. She happened to be the babysitter for an A.A. group. Her ex-husband was a drunk. She did a stint in Al-Anon and got recruited to babysit. Even after they broke up, she still loved those babies.

When she had to babysit, I'd catch a meeting. The meetings were held in a rather large church with an area for children. I knew sobriety was calling, I just wasn't willing to give in at that point. But I did enjoy those meetings.

We'd get there a few minutes early so she could settle in with the kids. Before the meetings, I'd rush over to the smoking area and quickly steam a Pall Mall.

On one night I was especially excited about going to the meeting. There was no reason, in particular, other than the fact that I liked the vibe there. Guess who I bumped into after grabbing some coffee? Fitzgerald.

He quickly assessed my appearance. I looked healthy. He was surprised to see me and slightly impressed. Since I was looking better, I lied about my clean time. The vibe of the meeting intrigued me, but I knew it was just another pit-stop. But Fitzgerald didn't know that. I felt a need to impress him, so I talked up my spiritual growth.

Then I asked about my old sponsor. Josh was still clean. Then Fitzgerald asked if I had a sponsor. I didn't, so I took his number. I had no intention on calling him. I toyed with the idea of him being my sponsor but knew it wouldn't work.

He called a few days later. I ignored him and felt angst when I stuffed the phone into my pocket. I relapsed shortly after that night.

About a year later, I finally surrendered. At the time I was staying with the "Sober Living of America" program. Sober communities generally bump into other communities at meetings. So, I bumped Fitzgerald again!

He quickly assessed my appearance. Absentmindedly, he nodded his approval. I was pleased. I could have lied about my clean time, again. But I was honest about my recovery, so I was honest with him.

As soon as I told him the truth, he shook his head. Then he asked when I was going to stop playing with my life. I walked away from the conversation without incident, which was growth within itself.

While stomping away, I thought, "Dude is just judging the book by the cover."

I felt a mix of emotions. My first emotion was anger. I was angry that he didn't believe in my sobriety. I was forthright about not being honest the last time we met. That alone should've been enough evidence that I was in recovery. Or so, I thought.

He chose to focus on the negative. I wasn't happy about that. I felt like he was being judgmental, which is what his peers at the community said about him. And I felt the same way, when I lived there.

I was angry that he wasn't proud of me. That's when I realized that I wanted his "approval." Something inside of me yearned for positive attention from this guy. That made me even more upset.

I've only felt like I needed approval from my uncle Walter. But a guy I barely knew, just because he was in recovery? That just wasn't me. That felt weird. What was happening to me?

I had to gain perspective. At that point in my recovery, I did a lot of self-evaluating. Later that night I locked my door and chain-smoked, trying to figure it out. We weren't supposed to smoke in our rooms, but I was still somewhat defiant back then.

It didn't all come to me that evening. But it was important for me to work through, what I viewed as a problem.

My initial thoughts were:

1. Fitzgerald saw me during my active addiction. He saw me running a lot. I was

constantly running from the police, since I stole from the stores across the street from his homegroup. He saw me running from the motel security also, since it's right next to the plaza where the homegroup is located.

2. Fitzgerald didn't trust that I sincerely joined the community. He felt like I was using them as a pitstop, and I was.

3. When I relapsed, he wasn't surprised. He still delivered the message of sobriety to me but wasn't surprised that I relapsed.

4. When he saw that I left the area and bumped into me at a meeting, he wanted the best for me.

5. When he hadn't seen me in a few months, then found out that I relapsed, he didn't believe I was honestly in recovery.

The last time I saw this man, I was proud of myself. I can remember how surreal it felt that I kept bumping into this guy. This guy saw me at a low point of addiction. Then he saw me tiptoeing with recovery. Until he finally saw me at the beginning of my actual journey.

When I first played the tape back, I realized that I only focused on his actions. I had to look deeper into the situation and get real. Why was I so emotionally invested?

Why did I have so much anger when dealing with this guy? Why did I feel like he "made" me mad? Why did I place expectations on this guy? People cannot "make" us feel a certain way. Our feelings come from within, so I had to figure out why he was able to "push my buttons."

It took over a year to figure this out. I didn't think about it every day, but I would revisit those questions.

I believe life gives us opportunities to grow. We face the same problem, through the many opportunities life has to present it, until we grow, then it is no longer a problem.

So, here's what I learned about the whole Fitzgerald situation:

1. I was jealous of his sobriety. Although everyone in his community didn't "like" him, they all respected him. I only lived with him briefly, but I did see him a lot in the parking lot where he had his homegroup. Prior to moving in with the guys, I frequented that particular meeting because they freely gave out cookies and coffee. They were in a drug hub, so it was expected that addicts would pop in now and then. Everyone knew that Fitzgerald was serious about his sobriety. In my heart, I wanted to be sober, but wasn't ready yet. I wanted what he had—freedom from active addiction.

2. We had the same temperament. He was a no-nonsense guy. But I was the same way.

His behavior reflected what I believed mine would be, if I got sober. Again, I was jealous. When I did finally get sober, my demeanor matched Fitzgerald's. I'm sincere about my recovery. I'm straightforward. I wear my sobriety on my heart and on my sleeve. I'm not playing when it comes to becoming a better version of myself. If I'm associated with someone and I find out that's not their goal—bye Felicia!

3. I yearned for a sober family. I needed his approval because he was sober. When I finally did get sober, I told him the truth about my past lies. I felt rejected when he was disappointed in me. I felt rejected when I felt like "the boy who cried wolf." That was because I knew he could relate to me. I knew that he was on his walk of betterment and I was also. I needed a friend in recovery that was no-nonsense, just like I was. But Fitzgerald didn't trust me, at that point. In retrospect, that's understandable. But I just wanted a friend in recovery.

I didn't like Fitzgerald's personality, so I didn't listen to his message. His message of spiritual principles were lost on me because I focused on the person. In all reality, I was jealous of him because I saw in him, a better version of myself.

Yes, I heard his message, every time he spoke. But I didn't listen. Like they say, "hindsight is 20/20."

Maybe if I listened, I would've embraced recovery sooner. Maybe not. I've asked myself a lot of hypotheticals about this situation. At the end of the day, I'm grateful to have met the man. And I've learned not to make that mistake again.

There are going to be a lot of people who "rub me the wrong way." But I learned in the case with Fitzgerald to focus on the principles. You can argue with the man, but not the principles.

Mr. Wonderful

My absolute favorite network TV show is "Shark Tank." If you've watched the show, then you should know who "Mr. Wonderful" is. Kevin O'Leary's demeanor on the show is anything but wonderful. I'm sure he's just playing the part of the "bad guy" when he lambasts hopeful entrepreneurs. But the guy has said some pretty rude things. His personality rubs people the wrong way.

A venture capitalist has one primary focus: return on investment (R.O.I.). After assessing the risk to reward ratio of a business, an investor needs to know the rate of return. If they believe it's a sound investment for their time and expertise, they will move forward. The cast of "Shark Tank" are America's celebrity venture capitalists.

After watching this guy for 6 seasons, I've come to a realization. I would partner with O'Leary on any deal. Mr. Wonderful claims to be the most logical venture capitalist on the show. He prides himself on being the only "shark" who respects the principles of money. And since money doesn't have emotion, he doesn't invest with emotions. So, I would partner with him on any deal.

I honestly cannot recall ever seeing O'Leary make a deal based on his emotions. But I've definitely seen the others do this.

Mark Cuban tends to favor kid-preneurs. Mr. Cuban's entrepreneurial spirit kicked in when he was a child. I've seen him devalue his expertise and time to favor deals with pre-teens that reminded him of himself.

Barbara Corcoran tends to favor women. She has invested so much with her feelings that it's a joke on the show. If there's a crying woman on "the carpet" pitching a deal, the camera zooms in on Barbara's face. It's a given.

What's interesting is how entrepreneurs avoid O'Leary because of his personality.

O'Leary seeks deals that are disadvantageous to entrepreneurs. He enjoys deals that grant him "perpetuity." In business this means "forever." A typical deal would look like this:

- I'm seeking $100,000.00 for 10% of my toy company. I make cute dolls that cost me only $2.00 to manufacture. I sell them wholesale for $8.00 and they retail for $15.00. Based on last year's sales and this year's sales, I'm growing at a steady rate. So, I value my company at $1.5M. But since I'm dealing with the "sharks," I have to offer them a discount at $1M. (Their expertise, contacts, money, and celebrity status equals value I can't obtain elsewhere.)

- O'Leary knows the toy industry. In 1999, he sold his software company to Mattel for $4B. O'Leary also knows the value of my company and the fact that I've already discounted it. But since he's a "shark," he attempts to gnash me, a little. So, he agrees to the valuation of the company and the asking price. He'll give me the $100,000.00 for 10%. But he also wants a $2.00 royalty in perpetuity.

- If I agree with his offer, O'Leary will have to receive 25% of my cash-flow plus he'll own 10% of the company. If we build the company to $10M, then he'll own $1M of the company. Let's say I had to sell one million units to reach that valuation. O'Leary would have also made $2M from those purchases. That's $3M from a $100K investment. **Wait, there's more!** Since the $2.00 per unit is in perpetuity, even if the company is sold, O'Leary has leverage with the new company! If they don't like that former arrangement, they'll offer him a deal to buy out that agreement. Needless to say, he stands to make a few more million.

That's an example of a royalty deal, using a perpetuity approach, which Kevin O'Leary is known for. If I were investing, I'd partner with him on this deal. If I were an entrepreneur? I'd pass.

Now, there have been times O'Leary has actually offered "good" deals. I've witnessed entrepreneurs totally ignore this man and partner up with someone else. I'm only including those entrepreneurs who obviously had a knack for numbers. Of those deals, they chose other partners because they didn't like O'Leary's personality.

The guy is super rich, so it's not like a lost opportunity will break the bank. However, my focus is on the entrepreneur, in this case. They chose to focus on the man's personality, instead of his sound business sense. In other words, his business principles.

Those entrepreneurs missed the opportunity to walk away with a "better" deal. When you're looking for investment you want the best deal you can get. The best deal is always in the numbers. Whether you "like" someone or not, it's not supposed to matter. The better deal is a binary choice: yes or no, right or wrong, better or worse. But we're human, so for many of us, it's difficult to leave out the emotions, even for a business deal.

These people didn't put principles before personalities.

What is your Passion?
I consider myself a student of life. Learning has always been important to me. Growing up, I thought it was cool to know a little bit about a lot of things.

They have a saying for those kinds of people. "A jack of all trades, master of none." Unless you plan on being on "Jeopardy," this isn't a practical way to live. At least I don't think so.

After some growth, I've realized it's better to specialize in a field. These days there are only a few subjects I'm passionate about. For me, it makes better sense to focus on those subjects and not much else.

My #1 passion is sobriety. Living sober has made me a new man. The new me lives a tonic life. The old me lived a toxic life. That's how I see sobriety: a tonic way of life.

This kind of life encompasses all areas of living: spiritual, physical, emotional, psychological and social. This is what I mean within this book when I say, "a better version of myself." The question that drives me is, "How can I improve who I am?" Living a tonic life answers that for me. This is my understanding of sobriety.

I believe words are powerful. What we say is powerful. By the time we verbally express a thought, we've already: thought it and felt it. So, when we say something, it is the 3rd time we've given "life" to that energy. Just think about that, for a moment...

The energy behind one word is powerful. We will receive two different reactions from the same person, if we tell them we "love" them today, then tell them we "hate" them, tomorrow.

So, when we use phrases and attach meanings to them, it increases the power of the individual words. This is why personal affirmations are so powerful.

This is why mottos are powerful. This is why slogans are powerful.

I have a passion for sobriety, writing, and linguistics. These passions led to me creating content like "Sober Slogans." Since I've gotten sober, it became clear that there isn't any material on the recovery mottos we use. No one has elaborated on the spiritual principles behind them. So, I've decided to do just that.

I plan to write books and narrate audiobooks on the subject. There's also a YouTube channel in the making. My goal is to simply provide context for our sober slogans. But this is my passion.

My question is, **what's your passion?** I implore you to find your passion.

I'm a recovering addict! I say that proudly, hence, the exclamation point. I'm in the process of healing, so I'm perpetually "recovering." If you're also a recovering addict, then you know that we've been given another chance.

It's a new life. You're a new person. Now you can do what you've always wanted to do. If you don't know what your passion is yet, that's okay. Being in recovery is hard work. Learning how to live sober is hard work. But, without even knowing you, I think I can help you find your passion.

It's a simple exercise, so let's get right to it.

When you're in a quiet environment, without distraction, I'd like you to do the following:

1. Close your eyes.

2. Now focus on what truly makes you happy. Don't worry about what you have to do to obtain it. Don't think about all the responsibilities you currently have. Just focus on what makes you happy. If your mind pushes in any other thoughts, then push them out. Your only job right now is to focus on what makes you happy.

3. Stay in that mental space and see yourself engaging. See yourself "doing" whatever that happy thing is for you. Don't try to direct the scenario in front of you, just let it unfold...

4. While you're "visualizing" this happy place of yours, "feel" it with your heart. Just allow the vision to unfold without direction but focus on how it makes you feel.

Our hearts cannot lie to us. If we're in love, our heart feels swollen. If our lover hurts us, we feel "heartbroken." Our heart identifies our lover, as our "happy place."

When we are passionate about something, our hearts will feel it. It will respond the same way whether it is a person or "thing." So, our heart responds with love when we find our passion. Our passion is our happy place.

When I go to my happy place, I feel full. Full of energy. Full of gratitude. Full of love. And at that moment, I feel like anything is possible. In that moment, nothing else matters. Overwhelmed with joy, I've literally cried before—in my happy place. That's where my passion lies. Where does your passion lie?

Embrace your Passion

So, it was a simple exercise, right? Simple but difficult. If you didn't get it on the first try, don't worry. Try again. Keep trying until the answer is revealed to you. And it will be revealed.

I'm not sure when I initially came across the exercise, but it worked for me. It took me several attempts before I was able to "feel" my passion. That's because I suffered from the "monkey mind." This is why I suggested you find a quiet place.

As soon as you try to quiet your mind and focus on your happy place, you'll "hear" all the chatter. Don't be discouraged. Push through it.

My hope is that you find and embrace your passion. I want your heart to swell and tears to fall from your eyes. I want you to be moved by it. I want you to embrace the feeling of love it gives you. Then I want you to go after it. If you don't, you'll be miserable.

Now that we're in recovery, there are no excuses. Recovery is about healing. It's not just about relapse prevention. That's the purpose of treatment. Even after treatment, we must continue to recover. We must continue to seek wellness. That wellness comes in all forms.

Practicing healthy principles are a part of wellness. Finding your passion is a part of wellness. Maybe your passion is knitting sweaters for cats. Maybe it's playing contemporary violin. Maybe it's creating content for the sober community. Whatever it is, engaging with your passion will make a difference. Embrace it.

During my active addiction, I'd think about who I would be, if I weren't using. I couldn't be that person because I was using. I was using because I had a spiritual malady. I didn't love myself. I didn't believe in myself. I didn't think my Higher Power loved me. So, it was impossible for me to be anything other than a crackhead.

I don't know how your spiritual malady manifested itself. But I'm pretty sure you felt the same way I felt. I'm pretty sure we used drugs for the same reasons. I know this because all addicts use for the same reasons.

But when we get clean we have an opportunity. We have an opportunity to be the person we said we would be. When we embrace our passion, we are truly living. If we are living out our happy place, we are truly living. Embrace your passion. Because by doing so, you are becoming the person you want to be. What's the sense in getting sober, if you're not going to be a new person? What's the sense in getting sober if you're not going to be the person you've always wanted to be?

Just by me writing this book—which is my first—I am living! I'm fulfilling four of my passions, at the same time. I love sobriety. I love writing. I love the power of words. And I love helping other people.

But there's even a cherry on top. I am becoming the man I knew I could be. I am doing what I said I would do. But I'm no different than you in this regard. I'm just using my tools.

Now that you're sober, you have tools that you can use to improve yourself.

You have an organization, (A.A./N.A./S.A., etc.), that you identify with. You have sober friends in your life. You may have a sober mentor, (sponsor), who is coaching you. You have a sober blueprint, (steps), you live by. You have sober functions, (meetings), where you can socialize. And you have sober resources, (The Big Book, Narcotics Anonymous, etc.), that can constantly inspire you. These are your tools for a sober life.

This is a healthy, structured life, for us addicts. I'm grateful that I have these tools. I promise, if you just stay the course, you'll find your passion. You just have to embrace it. You just have to live in it. Become the person you dreamed of, back when you were using.

Principles behind the Passion

Here's something interesting. If you look deeper at your passion, you'll see there's a reason it fills your heart.

Why does it swell your heart? Why do you feel alive when you're in your happy place? Yes, it makes you feel good. Yes, it makes you feel like a better version of yourself, but why? What is the principle behind the passion?

Essentially, I am a server. I like to help others. When I was growing up, I pretended to be "tough."

In certain ways I was, but I loved helping people. As a child, I took care of my brothers when my mother abandoned us, due to her drug addiction. I was the so-called "thug," who helped the elderly across the street. I even had a helping spirit during my active addiction. It's who I am.

So, the principle reason for writing this book series is simple: I enjoy helping others. Writing such a book speaks to who I am. This is why I am so passionate about it.

Knowing the principles behind our passions is empowering. We gain strength when we know what drives us. This can be useful when partaking a new endeavor, especially if we have a fear associated with the endeavor.

Doing something new scares most people. We tend to focus on our fears and then talk ourselves out of opportunities. Instead of looking at the value, we tend to focus on the unsavory "personalities" or nuances involved. This could be the people involved, or the elements of a situation.

Let's say a friend of mine asked for assistance. She volunteers at a homeless shelter. That might not be my thing. If I focus on the "personalities" of the situation, I may decline. But what if the principle reason for some of my passions is helping others?

If I focus on the areas that make me uncomfortable, I'll lose an opportunity to visit my happy place. If helping others swells my heart, then that's one of my passions. Not helping at the shelter denies me that passion.

So what if the building is dilapidated. So what if the patrons won't smell so nice. The act of helping them will fill my heart so much, it'll outweigh what I thought were negative personalities.

I mentioned this because fear holds us back. Fear chokes the life out of our passions, especially for recovering addicts. Don't let fear hold you back from growing into the person you want to be. If a thought swells your heart, go after it. Let the reason for your passion be greater than what you have to deal with to achieve it.

Choosing your Circle

I've always believed in being genuine about my intentions. I don't like "playing games" with people. I just don't have the tolerance. I'm the "tell it like it is" kind of guy. At times this attitude has served me well, then there were times it hasn't. At the end of the day, that part of my personality will never change. I don't want it to.

I've always been observant. I learn by watching. I'm especially good at watching people. Reading people is a skill that I'm proud of. If I didn't have this skill, I wouldn't be alive, today.

While in treatment, it was only natural that I used these skills. I thought it was important to know who was who. Who was there for recovery? And who was just taking up space?

Due to my assertive nature, I had a few "meetings" with the staff at the residence. Apparently, I was labeled as "anti-social," and at times "standoffish."

After my second meeting with the director of the program, they left me alone. Here's why....

I'm a firm believer in "choosing my circle." I don't like being chosen as a friend. I'm not saying it doesn't happen, but I like to do the choosing. Successful people vet their friends. I consider myself successful. If I choose you as a friend, I've done my due diligence. I've assessed a few things about you and believe a relationship can be mutually beneficial.

Being in recovery, we must be especially picky about people in our circle. People are fickle. Yesterday they liked you; today they don't. Tomorrow, they might or might not. Yesterday they were sober. Today they're using recreationally. Tomorrow they might be panhandling at Walmart.

Getting caught up with the wrong people—even in recovery—is detrimental. If the relationship is toxic, then stay away from it. They may "look" good. They might be popular. But none of that means squat if they're toxic. None of that means anything if you're putting personalities before principles. Choosing who we share our recovery with is crucial. Choosing what we share about ourselves is crucial.

We have expectations no matter what the dynamics are in a relationship. It's best to make sure your relationship is built on solid principles. If you're in recovery, you are living a life of spiritual principles. So, it only makes sense that every relationship is based on those principles.

Treatment programs are known for deterring relationships within the first year of recovery.

There's is a valid reason for this. If you aren't solid with your recovery, a broken heart can cause relapse.

In early recovery we're still learning how to cope without drug use. We're still figuring ourselves out. Without drugs we're forced to "feel," and we have to learn how to deal with our emotions in a healthy way.

People who don't suffer from addiction have a healthier emotional temperament. Drug addicts "deal" with life through drug use. We don't have the emotional capacity to navigate through life without a crutch.

It's hard dealing with life on life's terms, which doesn't include drug use. When we add someone else into our life, it's gets harder. If a romantic relationship goes awry, most newcomers relapse. If I'm learning how to deal with my feelings, then they get hurt by someone I trust, I'll seek solace. Most times a newcomer will find comfort in their drug of choice. It's understandable, but not necessary.

If the relationship is platonic, we still must be wary. Being in recovery is about wellness. It's about growing into a better version of yourself. The people you let in your circle are influential. If there are contradicting spiritual principles in a friendship, someone is going to be influenced. I'd rather that not be me.

The personality of a person does nothing for me. Not if it's not aligned with my principles. I'm this way in "real life," as well as on social media. I don't "follow" everyone, and I don't accept everyone's "request."

I check them out, first. I find out what their interests are. If exposing myself to their content is beneficial for me, then it's okay. I don't care what filter they use on their post. I don't care if it's an attractive woman. I don't care if I like dude's haircut. Based on their content, do our principles align?

I'm into subjects that aren't strictly sobriety related. I like all kinds of subjects, but I limit my feeds based on content. I don't want to expose myself to anything that won't support who I'm striving to become. Every now and then I have to purge myself. I'm not a strict disciplinarian, yet. But my point is simple: birds of a feather, flock together. Even if it's just on social media.

Choose your circle, wisely. Never put personalities before your principles.

Removing the Mold

I grew up during the "government cheese" era. (I can still see President Reagan, with a big "cheesy" smile, waving a big block of cheese on TV.)

We always had at least two of the five-pound blocks. My grandmother made the best grilled cheese sandwiches with that cheese!

One of my go-to snacks after school was grilled bologna and cheese. Most of the time, I'd forget to wrap the cheese with foil. Okay, to be honest, I was just lazy.

I'd put the cheese back into its cardboard box; and within hours it would dehydrate and turn brittle. The next time my grandma went to make sandwiches, she'd give me the look. The look also came with a lesson about waste.

On grocery days I'd help put the food away. There were times I'd shove an open box of cheese to the back of the fridge. We'd forget about it and open a new one. By the time I'd reach to the back for the oil-stained box of cheese, it would have mold on it.

The first time I threw the block into the trash, was the last time. After dodging an extension cord for 20 minutes, I learned to "cut away the mold." When she finally caught her breath, she expounded.

Basically, grandma asked, "Why throw away the whole, when only a part of it has been affected?" My legs stung, as I walked away, in awe of her brilliance. Now, more than 30 years later, I'm still using what I learned from that lesson.

It's important for me to align myself with like-minded people. If you're on a spiritual path to constantly improve yourself, we can vibe. If you like helping people with knowledge and your time, we can vibe. If you're egotistical, selfish, using drugs, and enjoy judging people—not a chance.

While I am picky about who I allow in my circle—once you're in, we're family. And like any family, we may have disputes. I'm a passionate person. I'm communicative also, so I like to debate. Not the yelling in your face, disrespectful kind of debating. But the true sense of the word: exchanging ideas through discussion. We don't even have to dress in our formal wear.

If you're in recovery, you're going to befriend all kinds of people. Some of us are assertive. While others are aggressive, or passive. Some of us are introverts. While others are extroverts, or ambiverts. And there's nothing wrong with. We've all come from different places, but we're all trying to get to the same place: the road to recovery.

Friendships are important to me. Relationships are important for everyone, especially the recovering addict. And we're never going to like someone, all of the time. Your friend is bound is piss you off.

If I'm your friend, it's a given. I'm opinionated. I'm assertive, and borderline aggressive, at times. Oh, and I like to debate. So, I can get on people's nerves.

However, I'm honest. I'm truthful. I'm loyal. And I believe in honor. But I will call you out if you're being unsavory. (You know, salty.) Maybe not in front of people, but I will call you out. I'm from The Bronx, what can I say? But I do value friendship.

During this process, I've learned just how valuable sober friendships are. In a sober friendship there should be a deep connection. Everyone in recovery can identify with each other, regardless if we had different addictions.

We can identify with the root cause of our past hurts. We can also identify with the struggle of addiction and the fear of becoming a recovering addict. If you're in recovery and you can't identify with a speaker at a meeting, then I don't think you've reached step one, yet.

My sober friend drank, but I smoked crack. My sober friend was functional, but I was a crackhead. My sober friend kept a good job, but I robbed businesses.

My sober friend is a woman. I'm clearly not. We're similar in certain areas, but different in others.

But our friendship is built on something deep. It's built on common spiritual principles. We've both suffered from the same spiritual malady that manifested itself through addiction.

We've both made it across the threshold from active addiction to recovering addiction. And we both have the lifelong desire to be a better version of ourselves. As long as those spiritual principles don't change, we'll always be friends. Our friendship is invaluable to me.

Unfortunately, some people are quick to toss friendships away. Some people choose to throw away the whole, instead of working on the part.

What I learned from my grandma, I apply to friendships. The mold only affected a small portion of the cheese, but I tossed the whole block away. However, I don't throw away friendships based on mold.

"Mold" in a friendship is anything that, if not removed, can and will, negatively affect the whole friendship. Whatever it is—it needs to be removed if you value the friendship.

If we are putting principles before personalities, then we have to address the mold. I don't care what it is. There is no topic "not up for discussion" in real friendships. There should be no "ostrich affect" in a friendship, where one or both friends "stick their heads in the sand," hoping an issue disappears.

As recovering addicts, we must learn how to deal with conflict in a healthy way. Drug use stunted our emotional growth. So, we have to strengthen our emotional aptitude.

Adopting conflict resolution skills is a must for our recovery. Having sober friendships is a must for our recovery. And though it may be true that my sobriety is mine alone, having a friend who's walking the same path, is a blessing. Having a friend who can relate to my fears of inadequacy, is a blessing. Having a friend who knows what I mean when I say, "One day at a time," is a blessing.

My focus is on sober friendships because of these common spiritual principles. But my message applies to any friendship that's worth keeping.

If there is an issue, address it, before it's too late. Remove the mold before it takes over the whole friendship.

When we put our principles before our personalities, we can salvage any bond. Friendships are formed every day. But those rooted in a common spiritual awakening? A friendship formed from a common tragedy? That's a friendship of a different kind.

Recovery from addiction is a story about tragedy turned into triumph. A recovering addict's story is the story of self-discovery.

It is the story of a lost, naïve soul, finding herself, in spite of almost insurmountable odds. Only after dying, then being resuscitated, was she able to learn the truth. A truth they all hid from her.

By keeping her blind, they were able to control her destiny. Until the day she rose from the dead to discover something quite fascinating: the very thing she clamored for all her life—existed within her, all along.

Having a friend on that kind of journey is priceless. Those are the friendships that legends are made of. Those are the friendships that legacies are made of. And we all need close friends on a journey.

You do know it's a journey, right? **Recovery is a journey...**

Recovery Is A Journey, Not A Destination

"Don't go through life, grow through life."

—Eric Butterworth

Self-Identity

So far, my journey to sobriety looks like this: Grady Hospital—Dekalb Crisis Center—My Brother's Keeper/Paula Crane Life Enrichment Center. This is the path I've taken thus far. I'm sure my future has more institutions in it, but the relationship dynamics will change.

Paula Crane has many functions, all of which focus on life enrichment. I was blessed to have sessions there while I resided at My Brother's Keeper. The sessions I went to focused on relapse prevention.

"The Crane" taught us how to identify the who's, what's and where's of recovery. This knowledge is crucial when making sober decisions. Knowing what a "trigger" is, empowers me to avoid **"co-dependent"** people, who may bring on a "craving." Understanding these terms—and many others in recovery—is fine. But who am I, in all of this?

Having an identity is the starting point for any journey. In every story we need to know who the protagonist is. Who is this story about? And who's the bad guy? Who is causing trouble for the protagonist? We call that person the antagonist. We need to know who's who in a story, to follow along.

It's no different in recovery. By the time I went to treatment, I knew I was a "recovering addict." I accepted that. But that was just a starting point. It was important to understand what that meant. By knowing who I was, then and only then, could I move forward.

Yes, I was a "recovering addict," but I needed to dig deeper. I couldn't just settle for a label and walk blindly into my future. I lived like that when I was an active addict. My future was going to be a sober one. To get there, I had to know who I was, in my own story. I was on a journey; one that would reveal my true self.

In any worthwhile story, the protagonist must change. Dissatisfied with their current existence, the protagonist must fight against and conquer internal struggles. Once victorious, they embrace a new version of themselves, while changing the world around them. My journey would be no different.

While in treatment, something became evident. On one hand, I had enough self-belief to be there. But on the other hand, if I didn't work on my negative self-talk, I'd relapse. I knew in order to survive outside of treatment, I would have to work on my self-image. How we view ourselves is rooted in our self-talk.

I wasn't the only one who knew this. Ms. Angela Wilson—my former counselor at The Crane—inspired me to work on positive affirmations. One day Ms. Angela gave me a mirror. Her goal was to help me change my thinking. She was assisting with my self-image.

She tasked me with a simple exercise. As simple as it was, I struggled in a major way. I was supposed to look at the mirror and say nice things to myself. I didn't do it daily, but I did it.

As addicts, we engage in negative self-talk, a lot. We tell ourselves that we're worthless, then prove it. Even when I was abstinent, my negative self-talk hindered me. I didn't think highly of myself, so I couldn't be successful.

In my twenties I threw away a music career. Instead of rapping to sold out arenas, I'd rap to myself in the mirror, while high on crack. My songs were lyrical bombs of self-hatred.

This memory came to me, every time I picked up that mirror. How sick was I? A man has to be some kind of sick to serenade themselves with such hatred. I knew I was sick. But I was determined to get well. So, I used those memories to work on myself.

I knew every time I serenaded myself with positive affirmations, I was undoing what was said years ago. I knew those words would undo the lyrics I used to brainwash myself.

During the dark times in my life, I was many things: thief, liar, robber, dealer, pimp, drug addict and alcoholic. I knew what I was, back then. I also knew in order to change; I would have to redefine myself. I needed to see who I wanted to be and strive toward him. That started with me saying kind words to myself in the mirror Ms. Angela gave me.

Without knowing who we are, how can we change? Without knowing who I am today, how can I become a better version? I don't think that's possible. That's when I realized how important it was for me to identify as a "recovering addict." That would be my starting point.

Many people in the rooms chose not to identify. And I've heard all kinds of logic behind this. Who am I to judge? If not identifying works for some people, then good for them. But I do identify and here's why.

Recovery—Defined

When I smoked crack, people called me all kinds of things. In all honesty, they weren't wrong. My spirit was infecting with self-hate. That mentality was depicted in behaviors centered around drug use.

I did what I had to, in order to get drugs. How could I get upset when someone called me a "crackhead"? I was a crackhead.

When I chose recovery, I stopped being a crackhead. I went from being an active addict, to a recovering addict. I never introduced myself as "Crackhead Jeff," but my actions did. My actions "spoke" for me. That was still going to be the case, but I needed to be proactive in my life.

I was choosing a life of growth, spiritual growth. Introducing myself with the word "recovering," invokes power toward my future. Recovery is returning to a state of health, or well-being. It is the path we take to regain what we lost, when we became addicts. It's the road that leads to a sober life. And it is a road that we HAVE to pave for ourselves.

What is recovery regarding our physical well-being? According to Yale Medicine, "It is the process of change through which individuals improve their health." From a medical standpoint, if you're in recovery, you are on your way back to a healthy state of being. So, every time I say that I am a "recovering" addict, I am claiming a state of perpetual well-being.

We can also look at it from another perspective. When we "recover" something, we are retrieving it. Let's use data as an example, for instance. When we lose the password to our email account, what do we do? We try to "recover" our password, right?

When we sign into our Gmail account, Google uses precautions just in case we forget our password. They set up measures to ensure that we aren't locked out of our account. We set up security questions. And we're asked for a "recovery" email address. We're even asked for a "recovery" phone number. "Recovery," in this instance, is used to retrieve lost information.

By using both definitions, we can conclude that: **recovery is the process we go through to retrieve the health we lost due to addiction.**

So, when I introduce myself as a "recovering addict," I am essentially reclaiming the health I lost. Spiritual, mental, emotional, and physical health. Of course, in addition to using positive affirmations, we must take action. Once the protagonist knows who they are, then they can move forward on their journey toward change.

Evolve or Die

I have a passion to be better. At times this passion grips me so tightly, I actually weep. I'm not talking about being better at my job or in my relationships. There's nothing wrong with improving in those areas. But I'm talking about being a better version of myself. Being a better me will improve all other areas of my life, which include work and relationships.

The person I am today, is better than who I was last year. I know this because today I'm sober; last year I wasn't. Honestly, this is the first time I've ever been sober. Not abstinent, but sober. So, I am currently the best version I've ever been, due to sobriety.

But I still want to be better. It's not that I lack gratitude. Not at all. My prayers are centered around gratefulness. I just have a passion to continue growing. I have a need to keep redefining myself.

The great spiritual teacher and writer, Eckhart Tolle, said, "Evolve or die." The reference here is aimed at humanity's thinking. More specifically, how we perceive ourselves and how we treat others. Mr. Tolle believes if we raise our collective consciousness, humanity will live better. I couldn't agree more.

I've heard this "evolve or die" reference before, from different perspectives:

- *Business.* If a business doesn't adapt to ever-changing markets, it will either go bankrupt or be bought by a bigger entity.

- *Species.* If a species doesn't adapt, it will be ravished by the environment or killed by a stronger and/or smarter species.

- *Personal Growth.* If a person doesn't adapt, they will miss opportunities, while others take advantage of those opportunities.

I'm not concerned with other people taking advantage of my missed opportunities. Recovery doesn't work like that. Recovery isn't about competition. It's not about comparing my clean days to your clean days. It's not about how fewer relapses I have, compared to yours. Recovery is all about personal growth.

I'm in competition with myself. I can either be my own adversary or ally. The choice is mine. I already know what it's like to be my own adversary.

During my active addiction, I was spiritually dead. Death begets death. Since I was spiritually dead, I couldn't respond to life. My addiction desensitized all life around me.

Now that I'm sober, growth is important to me. I'm of the opinion that if I don't evolve, in a manner of speaking, I will die. Looking back, it's clear how the process started.

My addiction started when I was just a teen. I didn't feel loved and didn't love myself. When my peers expressed their future goals, I'd make something up. I did that because I didn't believe I had what it took to "be somebody." I felt insignificant.

When a child believes God and their family loves them, anything is possible. Without it, a child grows up without purpose. Even in the harshest environments, if a child grows up with love, they can create a purposeful life. Without this foundation— even in the best environments—a child will feel empty.

I believe in the spiritual power of love. I also believe addiction is a spiritual disease. This disease can only affect those who lack the power of self-love.

People who love themselves are full, inside. Regardless of their circumstances, these people believe in themselves. Under the insecurities, behind all the tears and self-doubt—they believe in themselves. They have a form of self-love that enables them to avoid addiction.

They don't look for solace in the form of drugs. They don't drown their sorrows with alcohol. Even in their worst moments, they have enough power inside of them to get through. That self-belief is love. And that self-love is what separates non-addicts from addicts.

I didn't love myself. I didn't know how. I've also never met an addict who does love themselves. Rich or poor. Man or woman. Highly educated or intellectually challenged. None of these characteristics matter. If there is an absence of self-love, a person will seek it outside of themselves. Why? Because we all need love.

When you lack self-love, you have no power source. You have nothing to pull from. You have no purpose. Before sobriety I did have goals and aspirations. My goals were to get high. My aspiration was to become a "functional addict." But I didn't have "purpose." We can only gain purpose by having spiritual growth.

Since recovery has given me a sense of spiritual clarity, I can reflect. Being on the recovering side of addiction, I can look back at the active side of addiction. I never want to feel that absence of life again.

I've felt that absence of spirituality, that absence of self-love. My body was alive, but I was spiritually dead. Active addiction is death. Recovering addiction is life. If I don't keep evolving, I will die. It's happened before, so I know it will happen again.

I have a fear. I'm afraid of not constantly "becoming." I'm afraid of slipping back into that spiritual abyss. Even when the warm Georgia sun touched my face, I felt cold. In a room full of addicts, I felt alone. That was death, to me.

By choosing recovery, I chose life. By choosing recovery, I am choosing a journey that leads to self-awareness, self-love.

The Road Less Traveled

When I was in treatment, they told us only 1 in 10 people will be successful. Interestingly enough, I know of 9 people who have relapsed. Guess who didn't?

Recovery is a journey of self-awareness. If we're not ready to get to know ourselves, there is no journey. Think about your favorite epic movie or book. Strip away the world they live in. Strip away what they look like. Those are just characterizations. When we get to the core of it, every epic story has one thing in common. The protagonist seeks to find out who they are.

Your favorite character went up against many obstacles. The cool part is, they didn't even know what battles they would face. Sure, they knew there would be uncertainties. But they didn't know what those uncertainties would be. They just knew in order to reach their goal, they would have to push through. Our journey in recovery will be no different.

We will face obstacles. What are those obstacles? They are internal and external battles. Internally, we must fight against the old self-image. Externally, we must fight against triggers. These battles must be won, in order to continue on our journey. Again, the journey is one of self-awareness. If we are constantly "recovering," then we are always seeking the next version of ourselves. In order to reach each new level, we have to win unforeseen battles.

Internal battles. Throughout my life, I've had more negative self-talk, than positive self-talk. Today I'm improving my self-image, but I still struggle. Even in the midst of writing this series, I struggle. There are days I doubt myself. This internal battle manifests itself as statements some days. And as questions, on other days. I'm redefining who I am. So, it's only natural that this battle occurs. I must conquer my self-doubt. I must replace negative self-talk with self-love. This is the biggest battle that must be won. If I don't believe I am worth self-love, everything else means nothing.

External battles. Our triggers manifest as people, places, and things. By conquering our triggers, we can minimize our cravings. It's quite possible that I will always have cravings. My job is to limit those opportunities by knowing my triggers. For those times when my brain makes unsolicited associations, I must be strong. As long as I'm recovering, I will have triggers. This is the battle. Each time I conquer a trigger, I move forward on my journey. With every battle won I move closer to the next version of myself.

Just like our favorite characters, there is a goal for the journey. My goal, as a recovering addict, is to never stop growing. My story isn't a two-hour movie. It isn't a 500-page novel. However, my story does consist of twists, and turns, internal and external battles, setbacks, and triumphs.

I can't say how the journey will unfold. But that's the fun part. Not knowing how I will get there is exciting. And I'm okay with that. All I need to know is that I will get there sober. All I need to know is that I will constantly seek to become a better me.

I have been to prison. I have had many names and held many positions. But along the way, it'll be better to show than tell you. But I will say this: I have been blessed with a treasure no man can take. The treasure of knowing me, loving me, and seeking to further define myself. Along the way, I will be a benefactor of love, bestowing it upon those who wronged me, as well as those who have avenged me.

Alas, in the end, I will be the best version of myself. (Oddly, my journey reminds of my favorite character: Edmond Dantés.)

The journey of recovery is the road less traveled. The staff at Paula Crane literally said only 10% of the people would make it. Those statistics were quoted more than once. Of course, everyone claimed they would be successful. I can recall looking around on one occasion and thinking to myself, "Somebody's not telling the truth here." I refused to be the liar.

Please don't mistake my intentions here. I'm not speaking from a place of judgement. That's not in my nature. I'm not a "hater." Never have been. Never will be. I speak from a place of experience. I've been in treatment before and relapsed. I was of the 90% failure rate, more than once. This time around I chose to be the 10%.

But I've realized something. There are those who see recovery as a journey. Then there are those who see it as a destination.

Fearing the Unknown

I enjoy watching motivational videos. It's a daily routine now. Even before writing, I absorb positive influences to get me going. One day while watching Evan Carmichael's "Top 10" series on YouTube, I saw a video with Iyanla Vanzant. I love this woman's energy!

While speaking on being vulnerable, Ms. Vanzant touched on something that made me perk up. She said some people accept mediocrity because they can control that. These people perceive themselves as being broke and broken. So, there is a certain level of control in their life. They know what to expect.

I shook my head while listening to her. I was one of those people. During my active addiction I would hem and haw, but still choose to be a crackhead. I'd cry about no one loving me, yet I chose not to love myself.

I was used to the outcomes of my actions because I was the creator of them. If you've lived "the street life," you know what I'm talking about. I can't tell you how many times I've put myself in precarious situations, knew the outcomes, then acted surprised by the results. That's an addictive brain for you.

Ms. Vanzant further explained something I can attest to. She said some people don't change because they fear the unknown. Again, I was one of those people. I was used to seeing myself as a victim. I was used telling myself that I wasn't worthy of more.

I knew what to expect with that kind of mentality. But to strive for something better? That would entail a lot of unknowns. First, I would have to think differently. That meant undoing a lot of negative self-talk. That was hard work. I wasn't ready for that.

Who knew what would happen if I peeled back that onion? I'd have to relive those moments of my childhood. I'd have to question whether my parents loved me or not. I've been to therapy before. I knew I'd have to face myself. I wasn't ready for that.

Every time I thought about getting clean, I'd think about the work it would take to get there. I wasn't ready to start re-training my mind. So, I kept using. I was too afraid of what it would take to get there. I was too afraid of bringing up old memories, then having to work on those feelings. I knew what it would take, but I was afraid of the unknown.

One Simple Truth

That mindset changed when I accepted a simple truth. When I was on the 13th floor of Grady Hospital, I knew one thing. If I continued to be a crackhead, I would die. My disease already took me to "jails and institutions." The only thing left was death. I didn't want to die. I wanted to be a father to my children.

I held on to that desire from the hospital to the crisis center to treatment. Even though I was scared, I held on to faith.

Having sessions with Ms. Angela was fearful. My body would literally shake before our sessions. There I was, Mr. Tough Guy, shaking in my boots, as I walked across the parking lot to her office.

The brain cannot differentiate from a memory or a present experience. While recalling my traumatic past, I "became" the child version of myself. I sat there fiddling my hands, feeling small and vulnerable.

The fear of having to deal with my "stuff" was overwhelming. After one session, Ms. Angela said she might have to "pull back" from going so deep. We continued to work, but she chose other topics. Good therapy makes you peel back wounds. Good therapy makes you deal with your stuff.

My counseling sessions were exactly what I feared. This is the "work" I ran from, back when I was using. There were a few times I just didn't feel like "feeling." So, Ms. Angela placated me and allowed me to reschedule. Some days I just couldn't handle it.

My time at the treatment center was cut short, but I continued to work on myself. And the work was just beginning. I would have to do a lot of work.

The program was awesome. The therapy was great. I tried to keep the focus on myself, but when I looked toward my peers, their actions reinforced my fears.

People were relapsing, even while in the program. One guy got kicked out for smoking weed. Another guy was carrying guilt about not admitting he smoked weed. There was also a guy who got drunk, more than once.

I was scared. Some nights I'd wake up in sweat, from a "drug dream." Those were the worst. I didn't want to get high. At least, I didn't think I did. I knew if I went back out there, I wouldn't make it back. The fear of relapsing was making me sick.

I needed to refocus. I remembered something Russell Brand said in his book. Instead of focusing on "not relapsing," I would focus on "staying sober." I didn't have to worry about not getting high, every day, for the rest of my life. I just had to stay sober, one day at a time. That simple truth freed me.

Once I refocused, the fear of relapsing subsided. Instead of worrying about what I couldn't control, I focused on something I could. I controlled whether I relapsed or not. Sure, my future would have many uncertainties. When I was using, I faced uncertainties every day. One thing was certain, I was in it for the journey, no matter what.

All Aboard

After getting refocused, I still couldn't help observing my peers. Not everyone is in treatment for recovery. All I had to do was listen. When the staff wasn't around, I'd hear people talk. Some even shared their agenda with me.

I found out that for many, treatment is just a pit stop. People board the treatment train in waves. There are all kinds of reasons for this. Some people go because they're mandated by the court. Others go to keep a relationship. And still, others go to placate friends and family. They view recovery as a "destination," instead of a journey.

Maybe that's why so many people fail in treatment. Going on a journey implies something personal. It's a personal expedition, designed just for you. Recovery is about personal growth, and the journey is to get to know ourselves.

Having a destination implies having a specific place in mind. If I'm on a holiday trip to Las Vegas, that's my destination. I know where I'm going and when I'll get there. I also know what to expect once I arrive.

Recovery isn't like that. The journey of recovery is about growth. There is no designated place we go to.

We can't "go" to sobriety. We have to live it. We can't "go" to recovery, we have to grow in it.

This isn't like a cruise ship where the captain calls, "All aboard!" Sure, on my journey I'll meet a lot of recovering addicts. I'm sure we'll assist each other in our endeavors. But we're not going to the same place. My road to health is unique. We can't pay a ticket and travel together. But we can support each other. No matter how many supportive addicts we meet along the way, the journey is still ours.

We have to pack our essentials and start trekking. In some situations, we'll have resources. In other situations, we'll have to make do with the wisdom we've acquired. There will also be situations where we're just going to have to wait until the storm passes.

Embrace your Journey

I've chosen to embrace my recovery. I've accepted the fact that I am an addict.

Recently my mother asked if I miss "the life." For the majority of my life, I've lived as a criminal. That was the path I chose to support my drug addiction. It's natural to miss something you've done for so long.

I answered in the negative. I've lived as an active addict for over 30 years. During that time, I was the absolute worst version of myself. I was spiritually dead, meandering around like a zombie.

During that time, I would do almost anything for drugs. I've stolen, lied, and cheated for drugs. I've sold my body for drugs. I've pimped women, who sold their body for drugs. I've been to prison three times. I've been ratted on, shot at, and kidnapped. I've also abandoned all four of my children.

I miss nothing about being spiritually dead. I miss nothing about hating myself for my actions, but not having enough strength to change. I miss nothing about watching women sell themselves. I miss nothing about being the benefactor of those transactions. I miss nothing about wishing for death but being too scared to do it myself.

Once I accepted my disease, I made a choice. Like the diabetic who has to take insulin, if I stop taking my medicine, I'll die. I have a disease. I accept that. I've admitted that I am powerless over my addiction. I've admitted that my life became unmanageable. That's my truth.

This is the reason why the first step is about acceptance. We must be truthful about what our disease did to us. What it made us do. And what it turned us into. Once we can be truthful about those facts, then we can start healing.

I've heard it said that there are many roads that lead to recovery. I agree that there are many paths we can take, but the only road leading to my recovery— is my truth. So, I live in it.

I live in the truth that I was a crackhead. I thought like a crackhead. I looked like a crackhead. I smelled like a crackhead. I lived like a crackhead because I was one. But I'm not one anymore!

I live in the truth that recovery is a journey. It is a beautiful road—full of ghosts, goblins, witches, warlocks, and ghouls. But along that road is also, self-awareness, self-love, family, friends, truthfulness, honesty, and enlightenment.

I'll have to fight all kinds of battles. I know this. I'm excited for this. And I gratefully accept the challenge. I also know, now that I'm on this journey, there's no turning back.

Taking one foot off this journey means death. At least for me, it does. Recovery is my journey of perpetual well-being. On this road, I'll find my true self. If I step off this road, what is there? Death, my friend. Death.

I've already experienced that. So, I chose to keep traveling on this beautiful road to healing. Stepping off will only lead to relapse. If we're not working on ourselves, we are relapsing. It's impossible to do both, at the same time. Recovery is the process leading to health. Relapse is the process leading to illness. We can't do both, simultaneously.

Earlier I said my fear subsided. I'd like to clarify that thought. I no longer have a fear about relapsing. My fear of relapsing has been replaced with the excitement of recovery. To some, that might sound cheesy. I used to think that way when I saw people excited about their sobriety, also. But once you receive that power of love, you don't see it like that, anymore.

I'm not trying to get religious or esoteric. However, once we accept that we have a disease a door opens. That door is one of opportunity for change. All we have to do is choose to walk through it. Behind that door lies the journey. Yes, there are unknowns. Yes, the journey entails many battles. But it also entails lots of wins.

I no longer fear relapsing because I walked through that door. I knew behind that door was a different me. Who exactly, I don't know. I am still becoming him.

But I do know I'm a better version today, than who I was last year. I also know that next year I'll be a better version of who I am today.

How do I know this? Because I chose life over death. I chose to define who I am, rather than who I was conditioned to be. I chose self-love. I chose to embrace the journey. The journey of finding myself.

My hope is that you will choose the same for yourself. I hope a spark of self-belief grips you. I hope that spark travels its way through your mind, body, and soul. As it travels through your being, I hope it illuminates your consciousness. In doing so, I hope you see what I've seen. I hope you see that you are worth it.

I hope you come to the realization that you are so much more than you know. I hope you head the call and accept your journey. Accept the journey of becoming a better you. You deserve it. You are worth it. Okay, we're done for now. *Thanks for letting me share....*

Thanks For Letting Me Share

"A candle loses nothing by lighting another candle."

—James Keller

Knowledge is Power

Can you believe we actually used to use "smoke signals" to send messages? Imagine I'm on my mountain and you're on yours. The sky is clear and we're just catching up on old times. We're having a good time reminiscing, then the clouds roll in. What happened then? I guess we'd talk some other day.

When I was growing up there were still phone booths. (When's the last time you saw Clark Kent change into Superman in a phone booth?) Back then we had those heavy rotary phones in our homes. When cordless phones hit the market, I only made calls at a friend's house, since we didn't have one. Now look at us.

Since I grew up reading a lot, I fell in love with information. I didn't always use what I knew. And to be honest, most times I misused what I knew.

It is often said that Francis Bacon coined the phrase, *"knowledge is power."* I've learned that having information is one thing. But knowing how to use that knowledge, is another. That is power. Better still, using that knowledge to help others? That is wisdom, my friend.

Why we Communicate

I believe every human being has a need to express ourselves. Whether it's the child, crying for a bottle, or the deaf, "talking" with their hands—we all must express ourselves.

It's true that we grow from learning. But we must communicate our wants and needs within our environment and process the feedback, in order to learn. The more we learn, the more we evolve. The more we evolve, the more we seek to communicate who we are. And by doing so, we define who we are.

Living in the 21st century is such a blessing. Think of all the methods we use to express ourselves. My friend, DJ PDUB, streams "Live" mixing sessions on Facebook. My daughter distributes music on Soundcloud. Me and my mom video chat on Messenger. Me and partner attend meetings on Zoom. I share pescatarian dishes on Instagram. And scientists "beam" messages into the universe. We do all this to validate our existence.

If having knowledge empowers change, then sharing knowledge increases opportunity for change. We are in the Information Age. It is called that for a reason. The intranet birthed the internet, which birthed global connectivity. This level of communication changes everything.

Undercover Boss

I enjoy watching shows about business. When I have the time, I flip between 'Shark Tank,' and 'Undercover Boss'. The "Sharks" turn everyday Americans into millionaires. But 'Undercover Boss' has its own lane. The show puts top management in the trenches with regular employees. I generally just watch episodes about the brands I know.

These days I'm a pescatarian. But not so long ago, I was hitting the drive-thru at 'Checkers' for their "Big Buford." Although I'm eating healthier these days, I was still interested in the "Checkers and Rally's" episode.

The CEO visited three locations and learned something from each. Of the three segments, one stuck out for me. The boss went undercover as a guy who was thinking about franchising. So, he had to be trained. When he took his trainer outside to talk, the boss learned something. His employee actually had to train himself.

Then there was the manager. The manager was a yeller. You know those kinds of managers, right? The CEO wasn't happy about that; neither was the trainer. He felt disrespected. He said that he felt worthless when people spoke to him like that. But he needed the job to help pay for his mother's sickness. Little did he know, he was speaking to the CEO.

On the operations side of the store, there was a lack of quality control. Labels were misplaced and the food timers were off. The CEO decided to shut down the location, but not before speaking with the manager.

Still in "undercover" mode, the CEO called the manager outside to talk. Aside from being a "yeller," the manager was defensive toward his new employee. Come to find out, the manager didn't receive proper training, either. As soon as he was hired, his boss quit, so he became manager of the store. Without proper training, how could he train others properly?

None of the employees at that location were trained properly, so the CEO shut it down. Then he sent in a few superstar managers from other locations.

At the end of the episode the CEO asked his "trainer" to meet with him. He expressed his appreciation. The CEO explained that he was only able to make changes because his employee communicated with him. This just goes to show that having knowledge is power but communicating empowers all involved.

Virtual Meetings

I love my recovery family. By now, you know that I love meetings. Hearing "my story" when another addict speaks inspires me. When we share our journey, we help others. That is the ultimate wisdom behind recovery. When we communicate how we're making it through, we give hope to those still in need.

As much as I love being in a room full of recovering addicts, there's also my health to consider. I'm worse than a baby, if I get sick. If I sneeze, I panic. So, these days I do meetings on Zoom. It's a place where addicts can connect, from the comfort of our homes.

The best site I found for virtual meetings is: www.virtual-na.org.

I enjoy going to meetings in general, but virtual meetings are just so convenient. If it's your first time on the site, it can be a bit overwhelming. However, once you know how to navigate it, I think you'll greatly enjoy the experience. Let me explain.

The first thing you'll notice on the site are four tabs: Groups, Formats, Languages, and Weekdays. So...

Groups. All of the groups in this tab are what's available on the day you visit the site. Instead of scrolling down to the time of a meeting, just type in the name of the group and you'll be directed to its information. Let's say it's a Tuesday and you're looking for "A Spiritual Awakening." Maybe a friend told you about the group but nothing else. Just type in the name and you'll get the info. Filtering this way lets you know if the meeting is on Tuesday. And if so, what time the meeting is being held. Some meetings occur multiple times on the same day.

Formats. This tab has the "types" of meeting you're interested in. Let's say you're a newcomer in recovery. This is where you'll find all of the "Beginners" meetings. If you're looking for something gender-specific, you'll find a "Woman's" meeting here, as well.

Languages. This tab is self-explanatory.

Weekdays. The site lays the week out from Sunday through Saturday. Every meeting for that day is listed here. Under each individual day, the list of meetings starts from 12:00am-11:59pm. I use this option the most. My days are busy, so I catch meetings at different times. Let's say it's a Tuesday at 2:30pm and I want to catch a meeting at 6pm. Without using filters, I'll have to scroll down to "6pm" to see what all is available.

So, those are the primary tabs and how to use them. But I think a few more details should be explained.

Times Listed. You'll notice two aspects here that I find helpful. The time of each meeting is based on local device time. Since I'm in Atlanta, meetings are listed for "EST." For my sober family members who live in California, you'll see "PST." Also, for those with military backgrounds, 2:00pm is listed as "14:00."

The Search Box. Right under the time for each meeting, you'll see this box. I call this the "awesome box." Like I said, I usually just search by the time. Then I'll filter a little bit. Let's say I want to attend a 6pm meeting on Tuesday. The first meeting that pops up for me is, "Virtually Yours Worldwide."

The name of the meeting is intriguing, but I have some questions:

1. Is it English speaking?

2. Is it a Beginner's or a Woman's meeting?

3. Is video optional or nah?

4. Is it 12-step or Discussion?

5. Is it open or closed?

All of these questions and more can be answered by tapping the search box. At first, you'll see abbreviations. Tap the box and they'll be explained. Awesome, right?

Networking on Virtual

Don't believe for one instant that just because these are virtual meetings, you can't network. If anything, you can network even more! The meetings are held on Zoom. So, whatever device you have, there's a way to download it.

At in-person meetings there are three ways to communicate: raise your hand to get noticed, speak to the whole group, or talk to someone next to you. Believe it or not, all three of these are simulated on Zoom. There's actually a "Raise Hand" option, so you can inform the host that you'd like to speak. You can also communicate via text: either blast a public message or send someone a direct message. And of course, your mic and video are connected. You can opt to turn your mic off, as well as video. Although, some meetings do require you to keep your video on.

Going to an in-person meeting with 20-30 people is cool. But attending a meeting with people from all over the world! Now, that's exciting.

I currently reside in Atlanta, but me and my partner are both from N.Y. Not too long ago, we signed into a meeting in Harlem! I used to live in Harlem; it's a section of Manhattan. There were close to 100 recovering addicts in that meeting.

Keep in mind these meetings are global. I'm about to see "The Marksman." It has all the things I love: espionage, action, technology, and English accents. After the movie, I can't wait to catch a Zoom with the "OKNA Online Meeting." They're located in London!

Expanding your sober network is always a good thing. One day I'd like to take a stroll along the Thames River. Sure, it would be nice to post some pics of me in front of Big Ben. But it would be even better if I knew a recovering addict from London. If I popped into enough "OKNA Online Meetings," I would surely find a sober "mate" to have a "spot of tea" with.

When we share at meetings, we share about ourselves. A few years ago, I met a guy at a local meeting. He shared about his new lawncare business. I approached him after the meeting and got a job on the spot.

How many times have you approached someone after a meeting? Maybe you asked them to be your sponsor. Maybe you just wanted to thank them for sharing. You can do the same thing virtually. On Zoom, you'll see a list of everyone who's in that meeting. If you want to speak to someone, just message them directly. There are no limits to networking on a global platform.

Where's the Love?

Before I chose a life of sobriety, I'd go to meetings and sulk. There were times I attended meetings for parole. Then there were times I'd go to impress people. There were even times I'd go to get out of the cold and grab a cup of coffee. Yes, I had motives, other than recovery. But I kept coming back. And you know what happened? A seed was planted.

I kept coming back because I knew that's where I would find solace. No matter how much I struggled with myself, I knew I needed recovery. My life was on "drug addict auto-pilot." It was evident that I needed help. After 3 prison terms and many damaged relationships, it was just evident. But I still fought it. I didn't want to have to "live in the rooms." I'm grateful for those rooms today. Whether they are in a building or online, I love the rooms.

No matter what my motives were, when I attended a meeting, I'd feel the energy shift. I was living a dark life, but those meetings shined light on my soul. The theme song to my life could have been "Dark Times," by The Weeknd.

I lived in the shadows back then. The shadows of burnt up, abandoned buildings. And in the shadows of spirituality. But one thing was clear, recovery meetings held me down. I've only been to N.A. and A.A. meetings, but the love is the same. It didn't matter which one I'd go to, recovering alcoholics and addicts both showed me love. At the root of it, it's the same disease. And whoever doesn't believe that, just doesn't understand the disease of addiction.

Whether it was a stranger pouring my coffee or someone waving me over to an empty seat—I felt the love. Stuttering while I shared, knees knocking while I stared at the floor, stinking from not showering for days—addicts still showed me love.

I can remember sitting next to a pimpled teen one night. Boy, was he a sight. His body was a canvas of jailhouse and professional tattoos. He sat next to me in silence, with his hair spiked, eyes bloodshot and eyeliner running.

I nodded my head, as I pointed to the chair next to him. The kid didn't even respond. He just slurped his black coffee and stared at me. We both sat there, with our invisible shields protecting us. I gave him the side eye anytime I felt him looking in my direction. He mean mugged me anytime I gave the side eye. But he did bring me a box of tissues when I started crying. He silently waved the box at me, then stepped back into his invisible shield. We didn't even say goodbye when the meeting was over. But his empathy showed that he understood.

The love for a recovering addict is in the presence of other addicts. The love is in the heart of the addict who finally "gets" it.

Why we Share

When I was new to recovery, I didn't understand why addicts spoke about their past so much. Back in 1992, when I first started going to meetings, I thought they were just bragging. *Okay, so you got your life together...and?* I was a knucklehead back then. The truth of why we share is so much more than braggadocio.

Let's drill it down to the bare essentials. Recovering addicts share for two reasons: to help other addicts, and to help ourselves.

Helping Other Addicts. You have to go through some stuff to get to this side of recovery. You don't get a year clean, let alone a month clean, without some growth. The longer you live a clean life, the more you value sobriety. But you have to turn tragedy into triumph, first. You have to stumble, pick yourself up, process, grow, then repeat. The more you learn how to live sober, the more you can share your journey. And honestly, the more you will *want* to share. Not for the sake of bragging, but for the sake of saving someone's life.

My ex-sponsor Josh, yelled over my shoulder, "Jeff, keep coming back." It wasn't until more than a year later that his voice popped in my head. It wasn't until a year later, when I needed to hear something that would push me forward, that my subconscious pulled that moment forward. But if Josh didn't share that sober slogan, I wouldn't have had that to pull from. He communicated three words to me. Those three words empowered me to put thought into action. Those three words saved my life!

In all reality, the spiritual messages of a recovering addict aren't much different than that of a motivational speaker. Any decent "motivator" shares their "story." Regardless of the industry, this is a must. Whether it's business, health, or addiction, if you want to motivate people—you must share your story. You must explain to your audience how you made it. Three of the greats—Tony Robbins, Les Brown, and Evan Carmichael—have this in common. These men have their own unique "way" of expressing themselves. They have honed their communications skills, found a market for their message, and grew. But guess who has something in common with all three of these guys? The next speaker at a recovery meeting.

We share in recovery to say, *"Hey you, with your head down and knees knocking. It's okay. I've been where you are, right now. But I can tell you that it will get better. Might not feel like it right now but it will get better. Just don't use. Keep coming to meetings. Get a sponsor. Make some friends. Work the steps. It's going to be a journey, but it does get better. And how do I know? Well, here's my story. Here's how I got through."*

A message like this can motivate people. But the beauty is, we don't have to pay to hear it. We don't have to travel to some huge seminar. We don't have to take a Masterclass. All we have to do is go to a meeting; they're free.

I'm not saying there's anything wrong with paying for a message. I purchased Evan Carmichael's book, "Built to Serve." I love the book. And I appreciate his YouTube channels. His angle is for entrepreneurs, not addiction. But essentially, his message is spiritual. He motivates people to turn their tragedies into triumphs. His key word—his "power" word—is **BELIEVE.** Every video on his channel is for the sole purpose of motivating people to **BELIEVE** in themselves. That's a spiritual message, if I've ever heard of one.

The message of recovery is spiritual because addiction is a "spiritual affliction."

I met a guy from Albany, NY, back in the '90s. I caught a minor case and the judge released me to a treatment center. We would love it when Raymond shared. He was a funny guy. Funny, but brilliant! He had that "physical comedy" skill when he spoke. You know, like Richard Pryor or George Carlin. This guy loved to share his story and I loved to listen, and watch. I learned the term "spiritual affliction" from him.

He explained that even with two Masters degrees, he still disliked himself. It didn't matter to him that he had brains. Underneath his scholarly achievements, he didn't love himself. He had a spiritual affliction.

I always appreciated hearing the man speak. And playing chess with him. Now look, more than 20 years later, I'm still using a terminology I learned from him. That wouldn't be the case, had he not shared his story.

This is why we share; to help another addict. What we share today may not even sink in yet. It could take years before an addict uses what they hear. This is why it's advised that we "keep coming back." Today I know exactly what Raymond meant about having a spiritual affliction. I was afflicted! I know the struggle! Every addict knows that struggle.

Every addict has a love/hate relationship with themselves. This is the core of our spiritual affliction. When you're afflicted, it doesn't matter what your life looks like. It doesn't matter what you look like. If you don't love yourself, you will always find ways to put a salve over that scar. But no matter what you do, you will still be in pain until you address your issues. And if you're an addict, you will use, until you handle that affliction.

Once we choose to work on ourselves, we gain small victories. Those victories become the foundation for a new story. That's when we're able to start sharing. We share even while we're still in the struggle. We share despite the struggle!

Today I can tell you that I'm on the other side of that struggle. Today I'm sober. I live by the spiritual principles of recovery. The message that each addict ever shared, resonates with me. I'm not saying I'm cured. But I am saying that I am no longer afflicted. My affliction made me believe that I was worthless. Here's why...

My father was a heroin addict, so he wasn't around. My mother struggled with her addiction, until one day she abandoned me and my three brothers. About a week later, my step-dad came by, and left with his three sons, but not me. He left me by myself in the apartment. About a week after that, my grandmother rescued me. But on the first night, her husband beat me.

These events all occurred within one month. That month was the catalyst for my spiritual affliction. I felt worthless. I didn't love myself, so I turned to food then drugs. I sought solace outside of myself. Little did I know, the answer existed within me, all along. That's my story in a nutshell. This is the story that I share. How I went from tragedy to triumph.

I'm definitely still a work in progress. But that doesn't mean I can't share my story. I conquered my affliction. My higher power never gave up on me. The path to my redemption was recovery.

I received messages from my higher power through the stories of addicts in the rooms. I heard my story, in theirs. When they shared, they helped me. And I was told to do the same thing. So, here I am. That's what we do in recovery. We help others. But we also help ourselves when we share.

Helping Ourselves. I think every time we tell our story, we validate our success. Every time I share, I remind myself that sobriety is worth it; that I'm worth it. (What addict doesn't have self-worth issues?)

Sharing my story reminds me of the steps I took to get clean. Every time I hear it, I am more likely to keep moving forward. I am more likely to add on to that story of triumph. My story of triumph.

My story isn't much different from any I've heard. And it's probably not much different from yours. But that's okay. That just goes to show how much we have in common.

My story is one of abandonment, molestation, isolation, despair, fear, vengeance, sex, drugs, Hip-Hop, prison, pride, drug addiction, alcoholism, dysfunctional families, mental illness, guilt, spiritual atrophy, hope, belief, passion, spiritual ascendance, and purpose. And you know what? I'm proud of my story.

I've said in previous chapters that I love movies. My favorite movies are coming-of-age dramas. My favorite franchise is "Star Wars." Even young Luke Skywalker had to grow up—spiritually—in order to embrace "The Force."

I enjoy coming-of-age dramas of all types. However, I've found that I relate mostly to stories about teenage angst. That's because I was an anxiety-ridden, confused teen, myself. A few of my favorite classics are: "The Outsiders," "The Karate Kid," and "Rebel Without a Cause."

When I was a teen, I saw myself in those characters. I wanted what they wanted: to be accepted, to have family stability and to find my way. Sounds like all teenage boys, when you think about it.

In "Rebel without a Cause," James Dean plays Jim Stark, an introverted teen, who sought acceptance from his peers. He was quick to say he didn't want friends but dreaded being the outsider.

I spent my teen years and early adulthood in prison. You can only imagine the trials I faced. I liked to read. I thought having a library in my cell would keep me out of trouble. I did not. It only drew attention. So, I had to be violent, until my peers respected my "reading time."

The character, Jim Stark, didn't have a stable family. This was one of his desires. In real life, this was one of mine. I was abandoned by my dad, mom, and step-dad. I didn't have a relationship with my grandmother or her husband. In short, I didn't have any stability.

Life is different now, though. I'm no longer an angst-ridden teenager. Today, I'm stable. But I can still appreciate Jim's perspective. Seeing the cause and effect of his choices, allows me to reflect. I reflect and appreciate the fact that I've grown.

The same is true when I share my story. I'm only able to share about the promise of recovery because I've grown. Every time I share, I reaffirm my faith in sobriety. It's like claiming positive affirmations, but in story form. Instead of looking in a mirror and reminding myself that I am worthy, my story says it for me.

Recounting the events that led me to my sobriety, motivate me to keep pushing forward. Sharing my story with other addicts—especially the newcomer—reaffirms that I've made it to the other side of addiction.

The Other Side

Getting to the other side of addiction doesn't mean you no longer have an addiction. It means you aren't "using" anymore. It means you're in recovery. Once we've arrested active addiction, the real work begins. This is when we start working on those spiritual afflictions. This is when we start rewiring our brain. And it's a life-long process.

When we're in the rooms, we hear about recovery and sobriety. I've used those terms several times. But what do they mean?

Recovery is the process we go through to rewire our brain. We have to constantly expand our knowledge about addiction. The more we understand our disease, the easier it'll be to keep active use in remission. Examples of this are: following the 12-steps, going to meetings, and reading literature. For some of us, the recovery process also includes therapy, and treatment centers.

Sobriety is the lifestyle we live. This is the people, places, and things in our life. When you live a sober life, it includes recovery. When some people hear, "I'm sober," they assume it's just about not drinking or drugging. However, it's so much more than that.

For me, being sober is a spiritual-shift, a mind-shift, and as a result—a lifestyle shift. Being in recovery teaches me about my triggers. Living a sober life means I make choices to avoid certain triggers. Being in recovery teaches me about the functions of dopamine, and serotonin. Living a sober life means I make healthy choices on how to release these hormones.

Once we get to the other side of addiction, we're able to "feel." Drugs and alcohol masked our feelings. Our addiction turned us into one-dimensional beings. But sobriety enables us to truly become human. We learn how to process our thoughts and emotions. We also learn how to empathize. Once we can relate to anyone, without preconceptions—we have grown.

This is the spiritual ascension we encounter with sobriety.

Being of Service
I think the highest level of spiritual growth is servitude.

Iconic humanitarians that come to mind are: Nelson Mandela, Desmond Tutu, Mother Teresa, Gandhi, Buddha, Socrates, Oprah, Elanor Roosevelt, and Harriet Beecher Stowe, just to name a few.

Each of these people did their part to uplift global awareness. They understood their world and sought to make a difference. So, in their own way, they served their contemporaries and generations to come.

Socrates taught me the power of integrity and independent thought. I value all life—regardless of ethnicity, nationality, gender and sexual orientation. By honestly questioning my preconceptions, I've concluded that we really aren't all that different. We all just want the same things in life.

Buddha taught me that inner peace leads to selfless love. By meditating, we quiet the distractions of life. And in that silence, we gain clarity—which speaks to us in the language of love. Full of that love, we are able to be selfless toward other human beings.

Once each of these great men attained clarity, then taught others. They understood that they had a duty. Their duty was to serve. Once the student is ready, the teacher appears. That is until the student becomes the teacher, then the cycle repeats itself.

Both men were known for teaching difficult concepts through illustrations. Be it by way of real-life vignettes, fables or made-up illustrations, each man taught lessons through stories. We all love to learn through stories.

The thing is, both of these men had to attain a certain level of wisdom. Once they reached their respective heights of truth, they knew they had to share it. They had to share their truth because they believed it would change lives. And it did.

The "Socratic Method" of critical thinking is still employed by academia and clinicians. Billions of people can now access Buddha's teachings on meditation and inner peace. That is the power of sharing wisdom through stories. We all love to learn through stories.

Isn't this exactly what we're taught in recovery? Aren't we taught that our story is invaluable to other addicts? (Wasn't someone's story invaluable to you?)

You don't have to be a Buddha or Socrates in recovery, but you should serve. We should serve because if others didn't, we probably wouldn't be sober. I don't think I would be.

If Bill W. didn't share, there would be no Alcoholics Anonymous. If Jimmy K. didn't have A.A., we wouldn't have Narcotics Anonymous. See how that worked?

Once we get to the other side of tragedy, our gut tells us to share. Whether we listen or not, is another thing altogether.

And there are plenty of ways to be of service. Help with setting up meetings. Volunteer to read or pass around the donation baskets. If you have administrative capabilities, assist with organizing new chapters in your area.

Service includes time and sometimes money. The economy is tight right now, so many people can't spare money. That's okay. If you don't have money to spare, then share your time.

The easiest way to do this is by sharing your story. Talk to the newcomer at an in-person meeting. Share your opinion on a Zoom meeting. Stream a podcast. Launch a YouTube channel. Start a blog. Write a book. Just find a way to share your story.

You never know if what you say today will save someone's life tomorrow. Or a year from now.

My ex-sponsor told me to "keep coming back." Neither one of us knew that over a year later, that sober slogan would motivate me to push forward.

I haven't seen the guy since that night, but his selflessness really helped me. He reached a level in his recovery that compelled him to share that message. He just wanted me to heal.

And that's what this whole process is about, isn't it? Healing. Isn't that what we all hope for? After being caught up in my addiction for years, I wanted to heal. I wanted to find out who I would become without drugs.

It's more than just the drug use, actually. I know that. Recovery is about getting to the bottom of our addictive behaviors. It's about addressing the disease of addiction, not just the use of drugs. It's about rewiring my brain.

I still struggle, but not with drug use. I don't engage with destructive people, places, or things. I struggle with self-doubt. Even in the midst of reinventing myself, I struggle with this.

But my triumphs come by pushing through negative self-talk. And I push through in a number of ways. I might catch a meeting. I might vent to my partner, who's also in recovery. Or I might repeat a sober slogan to myself to get me through.

We don't just say cute words in recovery. Our sober slogans have spiritual principles. They have power. I live by these slogans, and others. Hopefully I've been of service to you.

Thanks for letting me share. See you soon.

Thank You For Buying My Book

Thank you for reading the first book of the "Sober Slogans" series. This is my first book and I have to be honest. I'm proud of myself. I truly hope it added value to your life. Just writing it added value to mine.

Please Review This Book!

So, did you love it, like it, or nah? I would appreciate it if you could leave me a review. Leaving an honest review on Amazon helps others decide with their purchase. You can leave your review here.

Need a Speaker?

Are you in the Atlanta area? If you're in need of an inspirational speaker, please reach out to me here: soberslogans@gmail.com.

Mailing List

Would you'd like to be on my mailing list? Don't worry, I won't be *that guy*. But I do have a few projects I'm working on. I'm writing the next book in this series, as well as a YouTube channel that I'm excited about. You might want to stay plugged in. If so, let me know at: soberslogans@gmail.com.

Okay, enjoy your day. Bless up!